# LEAN for SALES

## Bringing the Science of Lean to the Art of Selling

Seán Gillespie
Michael V. Testani, Sr.
Sreekanth Ramakrishnan, PhD

# LEAN for SALES

## Bringing the Science of Lean to the Art of Selling

CRC Press is an imprint of the
Taylor & Francis Group, an **informa** business
A PRODUCTIVITY PRESS BOOK

CRC Press
Taylor & Francis Group
6000 Broken Sound Parkway NW, Suite 300
Boca Raton, FL 33487-2742



Printed on acid-free paper
Version Date: 20160121

International Standard Book Number-13: 978-1-4822-5314-6 (Hardback)



**Visit the Taylor & Francis Web site at**
**http://www.taylorandfrancis.com**

**and the CRC Press Web site at**
**http://www.crcpress.com**

This book is dedicated to Sean's, Michael's, and Sreekanth's families:

Allison, Isabelle, and Madelaine Gillespie

Lisa, Michael Jr., Matthew, and Danielle Testani

Chitra Vijayaraghavan and Poorvi Sreekanth

Thank you for supporting us while we were all locked away in our respective rooms endeavoring to collaborate across two countries and three different time zones for over a year of weekends and free time while writing this book. Your patience, support, and encouragement are the only reason for our successful completion of this work. Our sincere gratitude and love goes out to you all!

# Contents

# List of Illustrations

# List of Tables

# Preface

Lean has a long and successful history of improving businesses by simplifying processes to gain operating efficiencies, thereby providing a competitive advantage. Almost everyone is aware of Lean's deep roots in the manufacturing domain, originating with the Toyota Motor Company where the Toyota Production System has become the premier operating model for manufacturing companies across the globe. Everyone in business should also be equally aware of Lean's successes outside of the manufacturing domain. Lean thinking has proven to be quite successful at dramatically improving processes in the financial and healthcare industries, as well as in many other business sectors and organizations across the globe.

While Lean methods can vary slightly from one industry sector to the next, it is the principles of Lean that make it universally appealing and widely successful across these multiple business domains. Foundational Lean principles include providing customer value, improving processes to help value flow to the customer, and empowering employees to redesign business processes to be more efficient and effective at creating customer value. When organizations embrace these foundational principles, they subsequently find success at providing unparalleled value to their customers.

So, why write another book extolling the many virtues of Lean? While every book about Lean provides something unique and novel, this book describes the Lean journey as it extends to a business area that is mission critical, yet virtually untouched by the Lean transformation. This book focuses on the sales organization, which until quite recently, has been largely insulated from the progression of Lean across an enterprise. One can speculate as to why it has taken so long for Lean to penetrate such a critical business function. Perhaps businesses have been successful by relying on the "art and know-how" of their sales teams, who open leads in new and established business relationships in order to sell their products and services. As long as the sales team continues to provide an acceptable profit and reasonable business growth, then there is no apparent need for a paradigm shift toward *Lean selling*. Unfortunately, this form of "we are good enough already, so why change?" thinking has kept businesses from realizing their true potential for decades. Hopefully, those visionary business leaders, sales professionals, and Lean advocates who read this book will see the need to shift their thinking toward Lean for sales thinking as they recognize the shifting landscape in business today that is focused on tangible returns, as well as the need to respond quickly to the changing demands of the marketplace and its customers.

This book describes how the proven "science of Lean" can be successfully merged with the "art and know-how" of the sales professional to provide a client with unparalleled sales service and support. *Lean selling* is the term coined here to describe a unique methodology that combines Lean methods with the more traditional approaches to sales. When these powerful selling techniques are applied collaboratively with a client, the sales cycle becomes much more efficient and the client experience is dramatically improved. This book describes these *Lean selling* techniques and provides a framework for the readers to apply these techniques within their own business and across their client base.

The Lean sales practices that are outlined in the book are time-tested and proven techniques that deliver profound results. Those sales professionals who have applied the Lean selling methods have dramatically improved their close rates, which is the percentage of actual sales delivered relative to the total number of sales calls made by the sales team. It is not uncommon for close rates to double or even triple as a result of sales using the Lean techniques described in this book. An additional outcome is an increase in repeat business engagements as customer satisfaction increases as a result of a Lean selling engagement. It is also important to note that while this book focuses on the sales engagement (or client facing) aspect of sales, which is arguably the core of the sales professional's job role, Lean selling also improves the efficiency and effectiveness of the overall sales function. In other words, the Lean selling methodology provides a framework for a sales organization to follow that provides a more efficient and cost-effective client engagement model. It also enables a prescribed methodology with key deliverables for the sales management team to use as their sales "success criteria." Accurately measuring the progress of the end to end sales engagement in relation to the sales team's "Likelihood to Close" ensures your organization's sales priorities and operating costs are properly managed.

Finally, we begin every chapter of our book with a quote from arguably the greatest scientific thinker of modern times—Albert Einstein. The purpose of these quotes is to provoke further thought and introspection on the part of the reader around the important points that Einstein makes about the virtues of scientific thinking, and in particular how these scientific principles can be applied within the field of sales. This book attempts to expand on these principles by providing a "how-to" method for Lean selling along with describing many useful techniques that integrate relevant scientific concepts and Lean practices into a more successful sales engagement with your client.

# Authors

**Sean Gillespie** is a leading authority on value creation and value delivery in sales engagements. Utilizing Lean and Agile tools and techniques he enables sales organizations and their teams to improve thinking and planning practices, and customer collaboration, increase close rates, and reduce sales engagement operating costs. A staunch advocate of listening to the "voice of the customer" and conducting an iterative sales engagement through factual data-led customer progression, as opposed to more subjective traditional sales methods.

He has enjoyed a 25 plus-year professional sales career working for 4 of the top 20 software companies in various senior sales and management roles. From his very first role in sales selling personal computers, Sean's focus has been based on developing strategic relationships with customers that enables tangible customer results. Today Sean works for IBM as a Client Value Leader in the IBM Systems/Software Division, working with IBM's largest customers and its internal customer facing sales and technical communities to facilitate client projects, with a focus on value delivery. Additionally, he advises the sales management teams on sales progression, success measurement, sales skills, and engagement enhancement.

Sean works across a broad range of client industries including banking, insurance, and manufacturing in the United Kingdom, Europe, and the United States. A native "Aussie" living in the United Kingdom, at IBM he has been selected to receive a Eminence Award, VP Award, and Equity Award for his achievements in delivering value to customers and his contribution to making IBM essential to its clients. As well his extensive experience in project value definition and planning expertise, Sean is a Lean Six Sigma Green Belt and Lean Black Belt.

**Michael V. Testani, Sr.** is a senior business transformation consultant for the IBM Corporation, where he leads operational and culture transformation initiatives across the global IBM enterprise. One of Michael's primary areas of expertise is helping businesses make a successful Lean Transformation. Engagements typically result in increased efficiency, the elimination of operational waste and lower costs, along with guiding client organizations to successfully adopting a high-performance culture as they make their Lean journey. Over the last several years, he has been helping to enable Lean and Agile transformation initiatives within the IBM sales organization. During his career, Michael has held several corporate leadership positions outside of IBM including vice president of engineering, plant general manager, director of manufacturing, and product manager, as well as serving as the president and general manager of his own independent consulting company where he has enabled several clients around the world to adopt Lean principles and practices. He is a certified Lean Six Sigma Master Black Belt, Lean Master, and Agile consultant.

Michael earned his master's of science (MS) degree in industrial engineering and systems science from Binghamton University's Thomas J. Watson School of Engineering, and he is pursuing his PhD in this same field. He has written more than 50 publications and presented them at well-recognized conferences and is the holder of two US patents. Michael has been an invited speaker at numerous conferences, universities, and industry events. He is very active in professional organizations and societies, including the International Institute of Industrial Engineers, where he has served on the Lean Division board of directors and is currently serving as vice president of technical operations. Michael and the clients he has supported have received many industry awards and recognition as a direct result of his consultation including the Institute for Supply Management Award (2013), Chartered Institute of Procurement & Supply Talent Management Award (2013), IIE Lean Best Practices Award (2011), IBM Vice-President's Award (2008), IBM Excellence Award (2002, 2010), Brandon Hall Award (2007).

**Sreekanth Ramakrishnan, PhD,** is a data scientist and client experience program manager with IBM Systems based in San Jose, California. In this role, he is responsible for using analytics to improve the client experience using proactive and prescriptive decision support for IBM's clients. In his previous role (2008–2015), he was a data scientist with IBM Corporate Learning based in Cambridge, Massachusetts. In that role, he had global responsibilities for facilitating transformation across IBM Corporation using actionable insights gained from organizational data. He is also responsible for facilitating organizational transformation through Lean and Agile practices.

He is a certified Lean Master and Lean Six Sigma Black Belt. He has won international awards such as the 2011 IIE Lean Best Practice Award and the 2012 Society of Engineering Management's "Engineering Manager of the Year" Award. He has also won numerous accolades in learning design and development, such as the Brandon Hall Award.

Dr. Ramakrishnan earned his PhD (2008) and MS (2005) in industrial and systems engineering from the Department of Systems Science and Industrial Engineering at Binghamton University. He has 10 patents, more than 100 publications in reputed conference proceedings and spoken at numerous conferences, webinars, and universities. He is a member of the Institute of Industrial Engineers (IIE), Society for Engineering Management Systems (SEMS), the Institute of Electrical and Electronics Engineers (IEEE) and American Society for Engineering Management (ASEM). He served on the board of directors of the Logistics and Supply Chain and SEMS divisions at IIE until 2015.

# Chapter 1

# Traditional Sales versus Lean Selling

> You have to learn the rules of the game, and then you have to play better than anyone else.
>
> **Albert Einstein**

## Art of Sales

When you look at organizations, large or small, one of the most business critical business functions is its sales department. Whether your company is selling products or services worth one dollar or a hundred million dollars, the sales department is the function that engages directly with your customers. They are the organization's eyes and ears to the outside world. They are also one of the primary standard bearers by which your customers will measure your company's capability by way of how they represent the products, services, and the value that your firm delivers. Oftentimes, when talking with an organization's sales leaders, you will hear a number of common complaints. These complaints from the sales organization are typically focused on low sales productivity, close rates, and limited sharing of best practices to improve the competitiveness for a product or service against the competition. Additionally, in today's competitive marketplace, sales professionals often complain about excessive quota targets, products or services that are no longer relevant to the market, or customers who just do not understand or care about the value proposition.

So why should your organization consider using Lean in sales? How will this book help you to win more sales than you lose? In short, why is Lean for sales different than the approach most companies take toward selling?

At its heart, Lean is a proven set of practices completely focused on its core principles of maximizing customer value and eliminating waste. Lean practices have been tried and tested over a number of years by some of the world's largest corporations, such as Toyota, Motorola, Boeing, IBM, and General Electric, to name just a few. In these and numerous other companies it has been demonstrated, Lean practices can be applied to every business and every process. Lean is not just about cost reduction and waste removal, but rather it is a structured way of thinking and acting for an entire organization to embrace continuous improvement. The hardened sales professionals reading this book will probably be saying to themselves, "So what?... How will this approach help *me* sell?" The Lean selling methodology outlined in this book will endeavor to answer that question for both new and experienced sales professionals, but first let's describe what a sales organization actually does.

A typical professional seller's primary job responsibilities include the following:

- Delivering client value
- Building customer relationships
- Gathering customer requirements to assist in confirming the value of products and services you sell
- Presenting the value of your products or services in a structured and professional manner
- Reviewing your own sales performance, and aiming to meet or exceed targets
- Closing sales

By using Lean selling methods in a sales engagement, a sales professional can break down a client's business problems into a manageable order of events, so that an effective solution can be realized quickly. Problem solving is arguably one of the most important skills in the field of sales. Another key skill that Lean will enable for a sales professional is the ability to align a customers business problems and goals to the products and services being sold. In sales, it is vital that a sales professional identify the decision makers who will agree on the capital expense required for a purchase; as well as understanding everyone's personal interest in the sale. Using Lean selling and leveraging actual customer data, rather than using subjective information, makes closing a sale much more likely. Lean provides vital decision-making and problem-solving capabilities for any sales professional. Additionally, it provides a framework for sales professionals to follow for confirming the value in a product or service sold to the customer in a efficient and effective manner.

In the last decade, there has been a paradigm shift in professional selling. This shift has transformed sales from the "art of selling" to more of a science. The "art of selling" refers to the art and know-how of the individual sales person, where good instincts, relationship building, and "sales acumen" are capabilities placed above the following of a sales process and making data-driven decisions. It does not matter what products you sell, sales today are more complex, involve more people, are highly competitive, and take much to close a than just a decade ago. Lean selling provides a professional sales person with the Lean tools and practices to sell scientifically and close more sales.

## The Compelling Need to Change Today's Selling Approach

One reason why sales organizations need to move their sales practices to a more scientific and outcomes-based approach is that during the last 5 to 10 years, there has been an emerging trend in sales. This trend is called "do nothing" syndrome. Most, if not all, sales professionals have fallen victim to this syndrome at some stage of their career. The "do nothing" syndrome in sales is an often lengthy client engagement that results in a customer buying nothing. In fact, it is the loss of a sale to the "do nothing" syndrome that is arguably one of the biggest problems that sales organizations face today. From a sales process point of view, your company has paid a sales professional for up to 6 months (depending on the length of your average sales engagement). The sales professional invests significant time to help the customer better understand the value of the product or services being proposed. Behind the scenes, when the seller is not meeting with the client, a team of people have probably spent additional time discussing and planning the sales strategy, understanding the key stakeholders, and agreeing on actions to continue to progress the sale. Moreover, the seller has built an excellent relationship with the customer and they provide valuable feedback to help the sales team qualify their needs, which gives them confidence that the customer is interested and intends to buy. Unfortunately, all of this work results in the customer telling the sales professional that they have decided to go in a different direction or that its buying decision has been deferred.

To lose a sale to "do nothing" is especially devastating for the sales professional because it is not that they have been outsold by the competition, but rather by some mysterious circumstance. The seller did not lose the business to a main competitor or anyone else for that matter. The client has simply decided to buy nothing. The "do nothing" trend comes about because a customer is not convinced of the value that a product or service will deliver. In today's challenging economic environment, it is better for the customer to keep their cash in the bank rather than spending it on a product or service where the financial benefit and business value is not well understood. In fact, the prevailing motto of business today is: "*If in doubt, then don't.*"

To use a Lean manufacturing analogy, the "do nothing" syndrome is tantamount to an organization that has just spent a considerable amount of time, effort, materials, and manufacturing resources to produce a product that is defective and not fit for sale. Sales organizations typically do not measure this cost nor do they even try to understand the reasons why their defective product was created in the first place. Roughly 90% of sales organizations just move on to the next sale cycle accounting for the defect by blaming poor product alignment or a personality mismatch with the client. They move on quickly because, after all, the world of sales is a "numbers game," which means the sales professional needs to get back out there to quickly identify its next deal and determine where their sales quota is going to come from.

## The Ill-Effects of the "Do Nothing" Syndrome

The net result of this lack of sales achievement can, more often than not, be attributed to the performance of a company's sales personnel. After all, it is the primary role of sales professionals to engage and communicate with a customer regarding their company's value proposition. Therefore, when a successful sale is not forth coming, it is a logical conclusion that the sales professional's approach to the engagement must be, at least in part, the root cause of the poor outcome. They may not have represented the product's value accurately, or they may not have met with enough stakeholders, or perhaps, they did not plan the sales engagement well enough.

In most organizations, the sales professionals are some of the highest paid employees within the company, yet the methods used to measure their performance have not changed in nearly a century. Typically, sales performance is based on the amount of revenue generated against an assigned target, or the number of customer meetings per week, and perhaps even the demonstration of sound account planning. The drawback with these sales performance measures is that they are mostly arbitrary and do not have a direct impact on how well the sales professional is delivering client value. These measurements are also not very scientific in their approach. Granted, it can be very difficult to utilize real data to validate a sales professional's actual progression towards closing a sale and their likelihood to achieve the company's set sales goals and targets. Most sales managers will readily admit; however, that much more can and should be done in order to objectively measure the successful progression of a sales engagement. Lean selling provides an extremely useful framework for conducting the sales engagement and calls for specific deliverables at defined milestones; which sales managers can use to monitor the tangible progress of any client engagement.

Frankly, the Lean selling approach is an ideal candidate for the area of sales, and it is particularly helpful to sales managers as a means for providing tangible milestones and deliverables along defined phases of the sales cycle. A sales engagement with a customer is, after all, just another business process. Of course, it can be a very complex process with a lot of manual and people centric activities; but as a Lean practitioner, it is a process like any other one that Green and Black Belt all over the world can process map, identify opportunities, and continuously improve. Furthermore, a sales professional's engagement with a customer can form the basis of repeatable practices that can be mapped and measured for continuous improvement. This book is intended to help sales professionals and Lean practitioners begin their journey of change by creating measurable data that assists sales in becoming more scientific in their approach to client engagements. Lean selling utiliizes actual client data to assist a customer in quantifying the real value that a sales team's product or service provides. Finally, by being more scientific and data led across an entire sales engagement, a sales organization is better equipped to combat the dreaded and insidious "do nothing" syndrome.

## Traditional versus Lean Selling

When looking to Lean selling for enabling sales organizations to improve the method by which they measure sales performance, then like any Lean practitioner, a sales professional needs to start by looking at the "current state" sales process by examining the traditional sales management model. As previously stated, sales management typically focuses on measuring a sales team's performance based on traditional measurements, such as quarterly achievement against sales targets, number of customer visits per week, and sales cycle progression against agreed upon sales stages and time frames. These stages are often graphically represented by a traditional sales funnel (see Figure 1.1). The stages of the sales funnel will vary from company to company, but typically they will cover the following broad phases for a sales sales engagement.

- Opportunity identification
- Initial communication
- Business problem identification
- Solution development
- Solution evaluation
- Negotiate the deal
- Close the sale

These broad stages are fundamentally gates used by sales professionals and their management to measure the progression of a sales cycle toward the ultimate goal of successfully closing the sale. Traditionally, a sales professional will break down their sales target in order to define exactly how that target will be achieved. The target (or sales quota; as it is commonly known) attainment is broken down and planned by using one or more of the following methods:

- By estimating the average sale size for the product and service being sold. This will enable the sales professional to identify the number of sales they must close to achieve their target.
- By calculating the "number of suspects" (customers not yet confirmed as an opportunity for the products or services being sold), and by

**Figure 1.1 An illustration of the "sales funnel" depicting the framework followed during a traditional sales cycle.**

estimating the ratio of the number of suspects that must be met in order to identify a real sales opportunity. Typically, a sales person might need 5 suspects to create 1 sales opportunity.
- By determining the "number of opportunities" (customers that are confirmed to have a business need and are interested in the products and services being sold) and by estimating the ratio of the number of opportunities that must be developed and closed to achieve the company's monthly or quarterly sales quota. Typically, a sales professional will need to develop 3 client opportunities to close 1 sale.

Breaking down a sales target and planning sales in this way can be quite useful. The prevailing belief by sales professionals and sales management is that if you talk to enough suspects then they can be developed into opportunities and creating enough opportunities should result in the achievement of a sales quota.

Unfortunately, the problem with these measures is that, more often than not, a sales progression through the stages of the funnel (the steps that convert a suspect into a real sales opportunity) relies largely upon subjective information and personal opinion. The progression of a sales cycle is decided based on the opinion of the sales professional and often times based on input from the broader sales team. Additionally, the sales strategy and planning process tends to be very subjective with next step actions similarly based on subjective opinion, rather than fact-based decision making. Although a traditional sales cycle will involve a significant amount of qualification to confirm these agreed upon opinions, and even if some opinions and assumptions prove to be correct, the level of detail that traditional sales qualifications go into is often insufficient to build a data-driven and fact-based client proposal. Traditional sales methods prefers instead to use industry comparative metrics, total cost of ownership (TCO) models, total cost of acquisition (TCOA) models, and other subjective approaches to build a business case for making a sale.

It is not the fault of the sales professional for following these over-used and ineffective approaches for making a sale. Traditional sales training around the world teaches sales professionals to talk with a client and ask specific questions pertaining to a client's problems in relation to a particular product or service being sold. Once a problem has been identified, the sales professional will spend the bulk of their sales cycle working to justify why their product or service is the right solution for the client. This approach to selling is why, when you review sales training agendas, they will focus on teaching sales techniques like questioning a client, asking closing questions, uncovering needs or pains, presenting a solution, and its benefits. Additionally, sales training courses typically involve working in groups to agree upon a sales engagement plan or tactics. Training typically focuses on reinforcing these skills through the role play of a particular sales scenario. In Lean selling, we refer to this seller centric approach as the "art of selling"; that is, it relies heavily on "soft" people skills versus a structured process for conducting an sales engagement.

For sure, every sales cycle must have some "art" in order to be successful. Lean selling certainly is not suggesting that "art of selling" be ignored or has no value in the sales profession. We are, however, stating that in today's highly competitive business environment that traditional selling techniques do not focus enough, if at all, on how to develop a sales engagement based on gaining a deep understanding of the customer's real business problems and how these problems impact their business. The goal of this book is to enable the sales professional to use a scientific and repeatable approach for leveraging actual client data that relates to a significant business problem and an agreed upon outcome. We call this approach the "science of selling," and the Lean selling methodology offers a proven, repeatable approach for combining the art and science of selling.

## Key Differences between Lean Selling and Traditional Selling

In Lean selling, we define the "science of selling" as the active collection of customer specific data that is personal and relevant to a customer's specific business problem and the delivery of an agreed upon business goal. For anyone who has been in sales for a few years, they have probably read the book on (or have even been trained in) *Spin Selling* by Huthwaite International or *Battleplans* by Valkyrie Consulting Group, LLC. The authors of these products are pioneers in this work that pushes the sales industry to focus on data collection as an integral part of a sales cycle, and while these methods are valuable, utilising Lean selling methods will enable customer specific data collection and utilization to a even higher level.

So how is Lean selling different from the thousands of self-help for sales and Lean Six Sigma books available today? Quite simply, Lean selling is different because, as you will read in this book, it will describe step-by-step how Lean's proven principles can be used by a sales force to significantly improve close rates by using a client's data in confirming the value of the product or service being sold.

## The Science of Selling

Lean selling focuses heavily on the "science of selling." This process centric approach is used because a sales cycle is just another process, and Lean principles teach that any process can be refined and improved. Documenting and mapping the process dramatically increases the ability for the sales cycle to be repeated and by improving repeatability in sales means *closing more sales!* By taking the traditional sales funnel stages used by most sales organizations and by adapting Lean principles to this selling model, then the funnel changes to focus on the following areas:

- Identify market opportunities—identifying potential value
- Select the right project—issues analysis
- Initial communication—client problem and goal statements
- Capability study—current process and data analysis
- Root cause identification—getting beneath symptoms
- Sales project storyboard—proposed future state process
- Close the sale and confirm client value—value realization

These stages in the sales cycle are referred to as the Lean sales funnel and are illustrated in Figure 1.2.

As a sales professional, one of the first skills that you learn is how to qualify an opportunity in relation to the product and service that you are selling. In Lean selling, we use these qualification skills, but make them

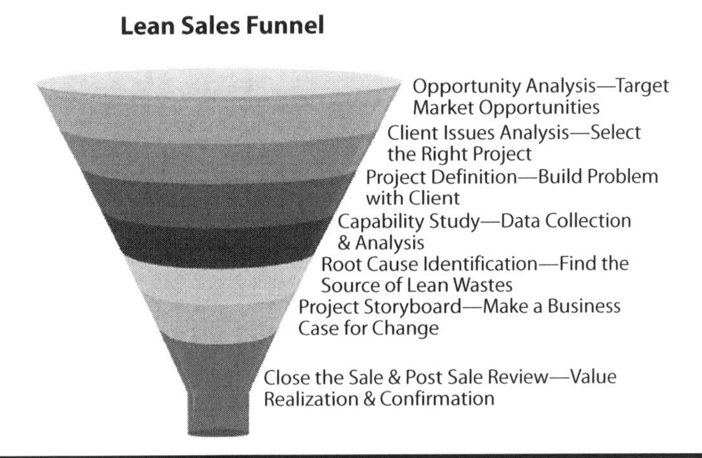


**Figure 1.2 The Lean sales funnel that outlines the framework for integrating Lean principles into a sales engagement.**

more effective by first identifying market opportunities that are the most likely to succeed. Additionally (and probably more importantly) we document the customer's problem and specific, measurable, achievable, relevant, and time based goal (SMART goal). Documenting your customer's problem and goal from the very first meeting encourages collaboration and begins the process of continuous validation. In other words, during each stage of the Lean sales funnel, the work products developed by the sales professional are reviewed and validated by the customer.

Additionally, a client's problem and goal statement puts a boundary around the project that you are working on as well as agreeing upon the financial cost of the problem and the time frame to fix it. If you cannot establish a project boundary, the financial impact of a problem and a time frame to fix it, then you probably do not have a sales cycle. With all the pressures and costs involved in running a successful sales operation, it is vital that sales professionals only engage in those projects that offer the best chance of delivering value to your business and to your customer.

## Applying Lean to Sales—Fundamental Principles

One of the foundational principles of Lean, and particularly Lean Six Sigma, is the equation $Y = f(X)$. In this equation, the "$X$" represents the variables within a process and the "$Y$" is the output of the process. In Lean selling, this equation is a foundation for beginning to work more scientifically and to begin collecting real data to progress the sales cycle. When working with the customer, the sales professional has documented and validated the problem that his or her customer needs to resolve. The problem in context of Lean defined as the output of the process ("$Y$"). As a Lean sales professional, we now need to spend time identifying the root causes, ("$X$'s") or reasons, that are leading to the clients problem ("$Y$").

We will spend a lot more time focusing on this equation, and its value to sales throughout the book, but for now it is important to note that the identification and verification with the customer of the root causes of their problem will significantly increase a sales professional's ability to close the sale. In fact, the majority of sales that result in a "do nothing" outcome end up this way, because the customer does not have faith that the proposed solution will fix their problem. Using the principles of Lean selling, a sales professional should spend at least 80% of the sales cycle focused on defining and agreeing on the root causes of a problem (as confirmed by the client).

This approach is completely at odds with traditional sales models where the norm is spending approximately 20% of the sales cycle defining the client problem and confirming its root causes.

## Process Mapping/Value Stream Analysis

In Lean selling, we utilize process mapping to document the customer's current and future state processes. This is because the more we can understand and document the current state process in relation to the customer's problem or goal, then the more we can identify the Lean wastes that might be causing the problem. It is the eight forms of Lean waste that allow a sales professional to build a financial business case based on actual client data. Additionally, in Lean selling the business case is built first when the problem and goal are documented, which is in stark contrast with traditional sales where the business case comes last. We recommend this approach to ensure that if for some reason the product or service being sold does enable a positive business case then we can close the sales cycle early due to the lack of confirmed value and move on to another opportunity.

Making a decision to proceed with a sales cycle or not to proceed ensures that the sales organization is not wasting money, people, or intellectual assets on an engagement that will ultimately deliver nothing. The additional value that understanding the current state process provides is that it helps to develop the client's future state process that is free of the destructive forms of Lean wastes. Additionally, in terms of the product and services that the sales professional is offering, it is possible to clearly articulate and show the customer how the proposed solution aligns with meeting their needs and time frames.

## Continuous Qualification

Every traditional sales cycle involves some degree of qualification, but in Lean selling the sales professional looks to undertake "continuous qualification." Continuous qualification is the practice of ongoing validation of assumptions with the client, and is based on the Lean principle of hypothesis testing. In the traditional sense, hypothesis testing is the use of statistics to determine the probability that a given hypothesis is true or false. In Lean selling, a sales professional works with the customer based on their problem and goal, and utilize data to continually validate (or hypothesis test) the facts pertaining to this problem. It is the act of continuous qualification that allows both the customer and the sales professional to have a high degree of certainty that they have identified the true root causes of their problem.

This book will explore the Lean tools and practices that can be used to ensure that continuous qualification takes place throughout the entire sales cycle.

As part of a sales cycle, a Lean sales professional has worked with the customer collaboratively to define a problem and goal. They have spent time to identify the critical *X*'s and have worked with data to continuously validate the root cause(s) of the problem that has been identified. Additionally, a picture of the current state process has been built as well as the new and improved future state process. We now need to present this information in a format that the numerous people involved the decision making process can easily understand and agree upon the value to be delivered. Traditional sellers use a sales proposal or price quotation. These are typically multipage documents with heading such as an executive summary, company overview, and solution overview. In the Lean selling world, these documents are considered outdated. In today's hectic business environment, a client no longer has the time to read multipage proposals that may or may not provide them with any real business value.

## Storyboarding

In Lean selling, we use storyboarding to take the reader on a journey that documents the work undertaken during the sales project and the value to be delivered to the client. The Lean selling storyboard uses pictures, graphics, and illustrations rather than writing pages filled with thousands of words that no one even has time to read. Most importantly, the storyboard shows how the proposed solution will align with the customer's goal ("*Y*") to deliver business value by addressing the critical *X*'s (or root causes) and removing Lean wastes from the client's process. Storyboarding is an extremely powerful Lean selling tool, and tangibly differentiates a Lean sales professional from traditional sellers.

One reason why the Lean selling storyboard is so well-received by the client is because the document is owned by the customer rather than the sales organization. It is owned by the customer because it is built in collaboration with the client and includes their data. The storyboard is designed from the start of the sales engagement and developed throughout the engagement cooperatively with the customer to qualify its validity. In working collaboratively with the customer as their trusted advisor, the sales professional has input into the story and assists the customer with their Lean techniques to identify the root cause(s) within the client's business processes. These are the causes that are keeping the client from meeting their business goals. The final storyboard that is presented to the client belongs to them and is personal and unique to their organization.

This personalized approach to sales is a really important distinction in Lean selling, and it is one of the key differences that makes Lean Selling so successful when compared with a more traditional sales approach. In the later chapters of this book, we will expand on concept of a Lean Storyboard as technique that helps every sales professional improve the way they communicate with their customer.

## Time to Value

In the traditional sales model, a sales professional typically builds a business case on the basis that the cost of the product or service being offered will cost less than the financial cost impact created by the customer's business problem. For example, a traditional business case is built for a product or service costing $1 that fixes a problem costing the business $2. Assuming the customer truly believes in the financial impact of their problem, then the acquisition of the sales professional's product or service creates an even bigger problem. This larger problem is a result of the fact that the customer has to gain approval to acquire the solution (for $1) and spending the money on this solution typically results in an near term spending event (payment is typically required within 30 days from sales invoice). Quite often in the world of business, the eradication of the financial impact of the problem (costing $2 in this case) can often take quite some time to return a benefit. In this scenario, the client is spending $1, but is still experiencing the $2 cost impact, until the solution gets implemented and begins to address the problem; which can take several months to resolve. In Lean selling, the time interval from product purchase to the customer's value realization as a direct result of the sale is called Time to Value (TtV).

In Lean Selling, Time to Value (TtV) is defined as:

*The time it takes to eliminate costs associated with the Lean wastes in the customer's current state business process and to deliver the improved business practices that enable the client's future state (typically, realized within a 6–12-month time period).*

Confirming TtV for the customer is vitally important in the today's professional sales world. Unfortunately, many customers have learned the hard way that time to value doesn't always deliver the financial returns as advertised. They have invested in a large number of projects that had an approved business justification but ultimately failed to deliver the financial benefits that the client expected. This failure to deliver value is one of the reasons for today's tough economic climate. Presently, funds are only released for projects and services that can absolutely provide a tangible return on investment in a relatively short period of time. Customers are rightly sceptical about sales organizations and their claims of favorable financial returns.

Accurately documenting the time frame to eliminate the Lean wastes and deliver the client's future state process is vital, as it enables a customer to calculate their return on investment in a 3-, 6-, 9-, or 12-month time frame. With a TtV time frame defined, the customer can now weigh the cost of the Lean sales professional's solution in relation to the net savings they will realize over time. In the following chapters, this book will break down the components of Lean selling such that a sales professional can begin to apply these principles as part of their everyday sales engagements.

# Chapter 2

# What Is Value? Lean Selling Principles

Strive not to be a success, but rather to be of value.

**Albert Einstein**

## Value—A Sales Professional's Favorite Word

If you have worked with sales people, or if you have ever worked with the sales department of any company, there is one word you will hear mentioned more than any other (apart from the word "quota"). For a sales professional, it rolls off the tongue like butter rolls off a hot knife. That word is: VALUE.

You will hear company representatives make statements, such as "*This is the value that our solution provides,*" or "*Our business case is based on being able to fix the customer's problem and deliver value to your business.*" There are entire sales training programs with content dedicated to identifying the best route to value. Most of these training programs are focused on situational questioning techniques; endeavoring to get clients to open up about their needs and wants in relation to their business challenges. The training typically involves taking part in situational role play scenarios to teach the sales professionals how to uncover these clients' needs or wants. Learning these techniques is important because identifying the customer's perceived problem is an integral part of confirming that your product portfolio or services can fix the customer's problem (for a fee, of course).

## Balancing the Art and Science of Selling—A Culture Change

Facts are indeed the life blood of any sales cycle. However, the fundamental premise of this book is that there is too much focus on the "art of selling" and not nearly enough focus placed on the "science of selling." So the question that we pose is the following—"Does having a powerful list of predefined questions help a sales professional define what is valuable to a customer?" The answer is that to be a successful sales professional, you must be able to ask specific and pointed questions to understand a client's needs. However, these techniques alone are ineffective and antiquated in defining value that is relevant to a customer. In fact, most sales professionals would agree that proving the business case for the client's acquisition of a product or service is one of the most difficult aspects of the selling process. Therefore, in order to gain a greater understanding of how Lean selling will assist a sales professional to define client value, let us first review some of the key integral principles we use in the practice of Lean selling.

## Lean Selling Principle 1: The Principle of Collaborative Giving

As a sales professional following a lead, you must identify a potential customer, and you may have even picked up the phone and convinced a potential customer to give you an hour of their precious time. So, what happens next? What preparation does a sales person undertake prior to that first meeting? Unfortunately, in many cases the answer to the question is that apart from finding directions to the customer's office, little or no time is spent preparing for this important first meeting. The sales professional is simply planning to ask their standard interrogative questions in an attempt to surface a problem that leads to a sales opportunity. This approach is used because most sales professionals depend entirely on the "art of selling" for their first engagement with a customer. They will lead with their bright personality, charm, and unique sales style, at least initially. At best, they will have a predefined set of "power questions" to ask the customer to assist in identifying a problem or need. Once a problem or need is identified they can begin aligning a product or service to the pain point that the customer is experiencing.

## *Do Your Homework before the First Client Meeting*

An important first step in applying the science of selling is by researching publically available information that will give the sales professional insights into a company's or corporation's business challenges as well as their plans to address them. This insight is invaluable to assist the professional salesperson in opening a conversation with the customer. Additionally, it enables a professional sales person to align their product and service offerings with the challenges of this prospective client's business. On the assumption that the majority of professional sales people do little or no significant research before attending a meeting with a customer. This omission would seem to be a significant lost opportunity. In Lean selling, this omission is viewed as a significant and critical error because doing your research is a vital component to gain the clients trust.

## *Gaining Your Client's Trust*

One of the most common challenges that a sale professional brings up is their difficulty in encouraging a customer to open up and share detailed information about their business challenges and/or business aspirations. When meeting a customer for the first time, it is important that from the very first moments of that meeting the sales professional must arrive prepared to "*give*". In Lean selling this approach is referred to as the "principle of giving". The "principle of giving" is founded on the Lean tenet of putting the customer first, and on a fundamental principle of human nature that people are more likely to be open and share with you if you first give them something of value. This principle means the sales professional must arrive prepared with something of value to give the client. It can be a simple one page document with a summary of the sales professional's understanding of the company's publically stated business challenges and goals, or a problem statement constructed from work done with similar customers. The key fact is that attending a first meeting with something to give and showing the customer your intent to work hard to get "under the skin" of their company.

When a sales team arrives to a client meeting for the first time, they must create an environment that demonstrates the "principle of giving". This approach forms an important first impression for the client and demonstrates to them how the relationship will progress. It is amazing how quickly customers begin to open up and share information as a result of a sales professional providing them something of value. Additionally, creating and sharing a well-written, one page customer specific document will significantly enhance the quality of your conversation. Subsequently, the quality of the information, data and insights received by the sales team greatly improves as a direct result of giving. After the meeting, this one page document can and should be updated with the new information provided by the client and then sent back to them as a confirmation of your time together.

## Give Something of Value, Gain Valuable Insights into the Client's Needs

The client relationship is now being built on the basis of how the sales person intends it to move forward. By utilizing Lean selling techniques to encourage open and honest collaboration that works towards identifying the root causes of the customer's business challenges (their problems) and their aspirations (goals), the sales professional can improve the sales dynamic. Gathering business facts in a "scientific" manner and utilizing a well thought out, organized and structured approach will significantly increase a sales professional's likelihood of success. From the very first interaction, it is the act of giving the client something of value that is at the heart of the engagement. Too many sales engagements start on the basis of taking information, and providing the client nothing in return. Sales professionals are taught to ask questions and take as much information as they can, and they often give nothing back—at least nothing of any value. No wonder it has become so difficult to get the customer to open up and share!

The key to this proven Lean selling technique is to always give something of value first. In doing so, the sales engagement will become truly collaborative and the relationship with the customer will be built on an exchange where the sharing of valuable information as the norm. In fact, where sales professionals apply the "principle of giving" the common complaint is no longer that they have difficulty in encouraging a customer to open up about their business challenges, but rather the complaint is often that they have too much information to deal with, organize and make sense of. Fortunately, Lean selling provides a multitude of techniques for managing all this information.

## The Benefits of the Principle of Giving

In summary, from day one of the sales engagement with a customer, the sales professional must utilize the principle of giving; utilize Lean storyboarding technique to encourage a ***continuous and collaborative*** relationship with the customer where the exchange of quantitative information becomes the normal expected behavior.

The principle of giving creates two additional benefits to a sales organization:

1. If a sales professional is utilizing the principle of giving with a customer, but the client is not collaborating by providing important information relative to their problem or goal, what does this tell you about your sales cycle? In Lean selling, we would look at this as a strong indication that suggests that your customer is not serious about this project or the customer is not looking for a value driven relationship. Either way it is an opportunity for the sales organization to opt out of the sales project early rather than waste internal resources on a sales opportunity that you will not likely close.
2. The principle of giving also enables sales management to measure the validity of a sales professional's sales pipeline. This is because the storyboarding documentation can form the basis of a milestone review. This review would evaluate the data created during the sales engagement with the customer and can provide greater insight and clear measurement of the opportunity's maturity level and likelihood to close.

## Lean Selling Principle 2: Continuous Qualification to Test the Health of a Sales Project

One of the key cornerstone skills of any sales professional is the ability to qualify a sales opportunity in context of the likelihood of the sales engagement to close. In sales, qualification tends to be an important activity that is done early in a sales cycle, and then again as the sales engagement continues to progress. Typically, a sales professional is of course qualifying that the customer has the requisite budget. They also must identify the key stakeholders and approvers, as well as defining the project timeline. In Lean, a cornerstone of improvement projects is hypothesis testing. Traditional hypothesis testing is a statistical methodology where the Lean practitioner seeks to reject or fail to reject ("accept") the null hypothesis. In other words, we want to validate that our assumptions and/or conclusions are correct or incorrect.

In Lean selling, hypothesis testing is an integral to our client engagements. The sales professional uses the concept of hypothesis testing as a continuous practice with a focus of continually testing how every client engagement is progressing. We refer to this concept of hypothesis testing throughout our sales engagements as continuous qualification. In Lean selling, our continuous qualification is not necessarily a statistical hypothesis test in the true sense of the word; however, it is an ongoing validation with the client that all assumptions, assertions, and conclusions drawn by the sales professional are always confirmed by the client.

Our intent of this method is to continuously test the health of our sales project utilizing real data provided by the customer. Ensuring that every engagement with our client confirms value in their eyes and progresses to deliver the clients desired outcome. Should a qualification test fail at any stage in the project cycle, then the sales team would typically halt any further progression of the sales project until the negative result is analyzed and sorted out. In Lean selling, the adopting of continuous qualification as a standard practice across your sales teams and your sales pipeline management process creates a culture and language within your organization, where testing the progression and understanding the health of your project becomes the norm.

This continuous qualification, in turn, allows your organization to walk away from spending valuable time and money on customer engagements that continue to result in negative qualification outcomes. Enabling your organization to focus more of the sales efforts and physical skills within the customer engagements that are most likely to deliver a financial return. A negative return for a continuous qualification is not necessarily a bad thing. It should be seen as an opportunity to revalidate and adjust your engagement to ensure that your proposal is on target to deliver value to the customer. Creating a culture in sales where all engagements are continually tested in the context of how your product or service delivers real value to the customer is hugely valuable to customers and sales organizations alike. As sales managers having this insight will enable your sales organization to considerably measure and improve the health of each individual sales project and your business health.

In summary, continuous qualification is the testing of the health of a sales project with a focus on confirming our sales team's alignment with our client's needs based on facts (i.e. the client's own data). In particular, a sales professional is seeking to validate continuously that his or her solution is aligning with a customer's problem or enabling a customer goal. From a sales management perspective, continuous qualification can be used to measure and confirm the health of any sales professional's pipeline and forecast.

## Lean Selling Principle 3: Value Is Personal

Value is personal, as it relates to an individual or a billion dollar corporation. A product or service for sale must solve a unique problem for the person or business purchasing that item. It is the impact of the problem or the achievement of a goal that the purchased product or service delivers, that creates the unique value proposition for a client. Lean selling enables a sales professional to personalize a business proposition in a context that is relevant to a customer's business problem and/or strategic goal. The Lean selling approach will be described in further detail throughout this book, and it will help the sales professional tangibly deliver a value to the client that is unique and personal.

## *Categorizing Sales Opportunities for a Repeatable Approach (Based on Value)*

As a sales professional, you will work with a number of different types of customers creating sales opportunities and running different sales projects simultaneously. When reviewing the total number of projects that you are working on with your customers, it is important to categorize them (prioritize using criteria). Are all sales projects the same? Do all sales projects require the same level of business case analysis or value led approach? Unfortunately, the answer is a definite "Yes and No."

The reality of the sales profession is that no two sales cycles are exactly the same. However, sales projects can be broken down into a number of categorical components. By breaking the projects down into two categories, the sales professional can identify the common components of the projects engagement. These categories are 'Reactive' and 'Proactive' sales projects (to be described further). This categorization gives the sales professional and sales management insight into the effort, engagement, and time frame that will be required to work with the customer on the successful completion of their project to the close the sale. Additionally, it assists the sales organization to standardize the resources required to deliver a particular product or service. By working in this way, we immediately begin our engagement with a data-led science of selling approach. Depending on your industry product or service and how your organization categorizes sales projects, you may not relate to the two basic categories: Reactive and Proactive Sales. However, please note that if you are not categorizing your sales projects or engagements with a view to confirming the repeatable deliverables of your engagement, then as a function of Lean selling, we would recommend this activity is undertaken.

## Defining Value—Intrinsic and Extrinsic Value

As previously stated, if you work as a sales professional or you work close to a sales department, you will hear a lot of conversation about value. In the past few years, sales organizations have become increasingly focused on delivering it. This is the primary reason that this book is being written and why Lean selling professionals need to spend 80% of their sales engagement time focused on the science of selling. It is imperative though, that we understand the definition of value. What is it and how is it defined in the context of a particular client and their project?

Personally, as sales professionals with 20 years of experience, we have never seen any sales organization define what value is in the context of a sales organization or a customer. That is, until now. Using the principles of Lean selling, there are two types of value; intrinsic and extrinsic.

**Intrinsic Value:** The *inherent worth of a product or service.* The value is based on capability that the product or service delivers "in and of itself." Typically, these are commodity-based products or services available through multiple suppliers—where the value of the item is closely equivalent to the purchase price of that item.

**Extrinsic Value:** The *portion of a product's or service's net worth to a customer that is agreed and assigned to it by external factors.* These factors are typically external to the product and service itself—they typically relate to the customer and their particular business. Selling extrinsic value may involve the customer making radical changes to their own organization to recognize the business value that a product or service can provide.

To further expand on the difference between intrinsic and extrinsic value, the sales professional needs to look no further than to the automotive industry. What is the *intrinsic value* of a car? Intrinsically, the primary value of a car that is derived from the fact that it gets you from one place to another. However, if getting from point A to B was the only consideration, then why do so many people buy expensive cars; like the European brands of BMW and Mercedes, for example? The answer is that car owners purchase their cars based on extrinsic factors. For example, a customer might buy a car based on the manufacturer's safety record, miles per gallon, or resale value. In fact, the automobile industry has become quite good at building extrinsic value into its brands and creating demand based on intangible external factors. These external factors might be the prestige associated with owning a particular brand of car because it is sophisticated and makes the owner look important. Suffice to say, there are factors external to the vehicle itself that determine the automobile's value as perceived by the consumer.

As a sales professional, selling a product or service using the science of selling and following Lean principles, the focus must be on building *extrinsic value* into the sales proposal that is ultimately presented to a client. Throughout this book, we will highlight a number of key principles that are the foundation for Lean selling. The principles are the sales professional's rules of engagement and are fundamental for enabling client value.

## Categories of Lean Selling Projects

In Lean selling, we categorize sales projects into two primary categories: reactive sales projects and proactive sales projects. Reactive and proactive projects are defined as follows:

### Reactive Sales Projects

1. Your customer has already identified their business problem or goal.
2. The budget or net operating benefit has already been confirmed internally.
3. The customer has identified and contacted a number of vendors to approach regarding a possible solution.
4. The time frame to have to project completed may be clearly defined.
5. There is a limited opportunity for the sales organization to define business benefit and value.
6. The delivered opportunity typically is based on intrinsic value.

### Proactive Sales Projects

1. The client does not have a project but may have some thoughts of a business area that needs improvement.
2. There is no project or budget allocated to undertake work.
3. The sales opportunity is reliant on the ability to prove value, improve a business process, and align your solution to the delivery of a quantified outcome.

4. The proposed solution may involve your customer having to change and evolve their business practices.
5. The delivered capability is typically based on extrinsic value.

One of the fundamental objectives of Lean thinking is about using Lean principles and practices to break down a problem or goal. Sales engagements are no different. By breaking down your sales engagement process into activities and subsequently categorizing the common components, a sales organization is able to standardize their overall approach, improve sales performance measurement, and improve how value is articulated to a customer. Many sales organizations leave the categorization to the individual sales professional and miss the opportunity to gain efficiencies of practice with the client engagement across the entire sales organization.

## Lean Selling Principle 4: All Sales Engagements Require a Mixture of Art and Science

It does not matter whether your business is selling widgets or if you are selling 100 million dollar jumbo jets, as a sales representative your selling skills will always involve both the art and science of sales. In Lean selling, we define the art and science of selling as follows:

**Art of Selling:** In Lean selling the art of selling is described as the 20% of interpersonal relationship activities (soft skills) required to build a strong collaborative engagement with a customer or business.

**Science of Selling:** The 80% of a sales engagement where the sales professional is focused on utilizing Lean tools and practices to capture customer specific data in the context of quantifying the cost and/or value implications of a customer business problem or goal.

### *The Art and Science of Selling—A Balancing Act*

From the very first sale in history, when two primitive tribesman met to exchange goods, they practised the art and science of selling. The art of sales would have involved one of the tribesmen utilizing their personality and powers of persuasion to convince the other of a need or desire to swap. Additionally, having been convinced of the merit in acquiring some animal skins in exchange for some meat, both tribesmen would have to utilize the science of sales to measure whether the exchange of two skins for one big lump of meat was a fair exchange. Today, the principles of sales have not changed; they are the same today as they were when the tribesmen exchanged skins for meat. It is, however, the main contention of this book that over the years as people, businesses, and industry in general have matured and become more and more complex, as has the field of sales.

Evolution creates the need for sales professionals to spend more time working to simplify complexity, influence stakeholders and break down the barriers to success. So, how does a sales professional break down complexity? By utilizing an approach that is more scientific, methodical and repeatable in the sales engagement with a client.

## Illustrating This Balancing Act

An excellent example of how the mix of art and science of selling has changed sales over time comes from the computer industry. In the late 1970s and early 1980s the computer industry was in its infancy, but a change began with the advent of the personal computer (PC) in the 1980s. That change is still taking place today with the advent of smart phones. However, back in the late 1970s and early 1980s computers were new. Certainly the concept of a PC being utilized in any business was brand new, if not unheard of. At that time computers in business were big boxes that sat in computer rooms being maintained by an army of IT staff.

If you were a sales professional during that time, imagine the talking points that you would have when you went to visit customers to sell them on the value to their businesses by investing in PCs. You would be talking to them about amazing chip technology, math coprocessors, and software such as VisiCalc the worlds first spread sheet, as well as something called a word processor to replace the typewriter. In this interaction, the sales professional was typically the expert when they walked into the room to meet with their customer. The point being that the art of selling, in the form of person-to-person relationships, was more than enough to substantiate the need or want for a business to buy a PC. This was because the sales professional at that time was the expert in this emerging market of PCs. The vast majority of customers had little understanding computers or the value that they could deliver to a business. The value that a PC could deliver to a business was typically accepted with little requirement for scientific proof. The relationship between a sales professional and customer was based on trust and the sales professionals computer subject matter expertise. This does not mean that the sales professional did not need to utilize the science of selling with the customer. After all, the customer still had to make decisions about the cost of the solution, in comparison to the value of the features delivered, and the additional services provided.

Moving forward 20–30 years, as the computer industry has matured today, everybody carries a smart phone capable of 1000 times more than the first PC. During this time, the subject matter expertise for the most part has shifted from the sales industry to the customer. Over time this increased market maturity has resulted in the customer developing "in market" business and industry specific expertise, which creates a paradigm shift for sales where the customer has much more knowledge and control. The sales professional in the computer industry is just one example of how the subject matter expertise (SME) has shifted from sales to the customer. As a market matures over time and transitions from new and emerging to stable and mature, so does the level of subject matter expertise shift from sales to the consumer. This paradigm is not just limited to the IT industry and impacts most if not all market segments. It is this shift that has dramatically changed the skills required in the sales profession over time. The result is sales needing to have an iterative, repeatable approach to scientifically engage with chosen markets and customers. A change that focuses on utilising real customer data to justify the sale of a product or service to a SME customer. In Lean selling we approach all sales engagement with a goal of spending 80% of our sales engagement focused on the science of sales working with real data and 20% of our time focused focused on the art of sales. This is in direct contrast to the traditional sales which is typically the opposite.

## The Shift to the Science of Selling, without Compromising the Art

This shift in client maturity has created a significant challenge for the sales industry in general. In particular, how can we educate and train our sales force to spend more time working to identify real data related to the customer's problem? How can we engage customer facing teams to work with SME customers, building the business case needed to successfully sell a product or service? Creating a proposal that is based on tangible data and that delivers value relevant to a company or individual becomes the critical part of a sales professional's role.

Like with any paradigm shift, not everybody notices that the rules have changed. In fact, we would argue that there are still sales departments out there today that still work on the premise that the art of sales is more important than the science of sales. In fact, you may be reading this book because you may currently work for an organization where the art takes precedence over the science. Recognizing the fact that 80% of a sales professional's job description is about working with facts and data is vitally important to effect a change of focus. Helping your customer break down a problem and or goal in methodical, repeatable manner is the critical success factor. As a sales professional you do this with one objective in mind, and that is the identification of the root cause/causes of the customer's problem. Having identified the problem as a sales professional you will quantify to your customer how your solution or services will align to fix the customer's problem or assist in the delivery of a goal.

In summary, all sales engagements require a mix of art and science. In the modern business world where customers are typically the SMEs, utilizing the science of selling to confirm the business outcome is a vital ingredient of sales success. In Lean selling, we recommend 20% of your engagements be focused on the art of selling and 80% of your engagements be focused on the science of selling.

## Lean Selling Principle 5: Document Your Customer Business Process to Enable Root Cause Identification

### *Putting on Your "Lean Thinking Cap"—Understanding Processes*

As a sales professional, you are taught very early on in your career to focus your questioning on the identification of your potential client's problem or goal. In particular, you are searching for a problem that your product or service can address effectively and efficiently (when compared to your competitor's products). This is the age old approach to sales and these techniques are actively practiced and taught in many top 500 companies today. In practice, this approach can work and can result in the closure of a sale.

From the Lean selling perspective, this approach is old and inefficient due to the many reasons we have already outlined and discussed. Mainly, it is outdated because it makes the assumption that the customer's account of the problem is the root cause, when in reality it could just be a symptom. In Lean selling, the sales professional sees the identification of a customer's problem or goal as the beginning of a sales cycle. What happens next includes a deeper understanding and documenting the process in the context of the problem. By working at a process level, we are able to confirm root cause and use the science of selling to build a more compelling business case and close more sales.

When you break down your client's business operations, there are both core processes and enabling processes. It does not matter whether your customer's business is small, large, or global—business processes (core and enabling) are at the heart of their business. How well and efficient business processes operate can have a significant impact on your customer's ability to operate, produce products, deliver services, and maintain profitability. When using Lean as a tool to scientifically improve sales, the primary focus is in documenting and understanding the end-to-end process that the customer wants to improve.

As an example, when talking to a client in relation to a specific problem we are studying, we look at the process from an end-to-end perspective, or from A to B (see Figure 2.1). In particular we are asking a very specific question, "Does the process work?"

Typically the processes of a business always work. After all, your business would not exist if your processes did not function at all. as you would not be able to offer your services. The question, once you look a little closer at a customer problem and the associated A to B process is, "Does it work well?" The answer is then often "NO!" or "NOT VERY WELL."

When you look at the process in more detail, you (and your client in turn) will find that the business function or process (Figure 2.2) is only

**Figure 2.1 Process depiction from point A to point B.**

**Figure 2.2 Process depiction from point A to point B indicating manual functions (buckets) necessary to make a business process work.**

enabled through manual engagement of staff and the utilization of other business practices. These are all sources of Lean wastes and can have a significant effect in creating your client's problem.

## *Helping to Define Y = f(X) for the Client*

It is the "buckets" of a process that are the "*X's*" which represent the inputs and process variables that result in the "*Y*" output variable (as discussed in Chapter 1). In other words, we are working with the Lean equation $Y = f(X)$. But why would identifying the "*X*'s" be important to a sales professional? After all, a sales professionals job is to sell and not become consultants. Sales Managers at this point often pushes back and says the organization's sales professionals are probably far too busy to do this. But they are missing a really important fact. In order to be successful today more time must be spent understanding a clients unique problems.

We have already discussed the importance of value in sales engagements, and introduced the idea of extrinsic value. If you are a sales professional or working with a team of sales people, and you are not working with a customer to identify "*X*"s that are creating a client's problem (Output "*Y*"), then you are missing the opportunity to build a substantive business case focused on aligning your product or service to solve the customer's problem and deliver extrinsic value.

By having clear insight into the customer's process and the "*X*"s that are creating a customer problem or impacting the achievement of a business goal, a sales professional can build a superior business case that is based on real facts that relate to the client and make the effect of the problem personal. We are able to confirm using customer specific data (science of selling) the impact that the "*X*"s are having on a customer and their day-to-day operations and staff. Additionally, there is a versatile toolbox of standardized Lean tools and techniques available for use by the sales professional to allow you to accurately confirm the financial impact of the root cause of the "*X*"s.

In summary, documenting your customer business process enables a sales professional to document the root causes that are creating a customer problem or impacting the delivery of a business goal. It enables the ability to personalize your product or service value.

## Lean Selling Principle 6: Align Your Product or Service to the Customer Problem and Goal

Working with customers at a process level is a fundamental principle of this book and Lean selling in general. It is vital, as it enables the professional seller to identify root causes creating a customer's business problem or inhibiting the achievement of a business goal. It is important, though, for another reason. At the end of the day, this book is about selling and increasing sales. Improving the sales team's engagement with a customer and gaining better insight of how effective your sales team is in engaging with your customers is vital to sales success. So, how does understanding a customer's process make the product or service that you are selling more valuable and enable you to beat the competition?

The answer is simple. With a detailed understanding of the waste in the customer's process, it enables the sales organization to align the capabilities and outcomes of your product and service such that it is possible to demonstrate how waste can be reduced and preferably eliminated. In particular, it enables a sales organization to align the core value creating components or competencies of the product and service that will eliminate the customers waste and successfully enable the delivery of the customers outcomes. This is a game changer, as for the first time a sales professional can confirm to the clients the specific business outcomes that they will deliver to enable the client to achieve their business goals (Figure 2.3).

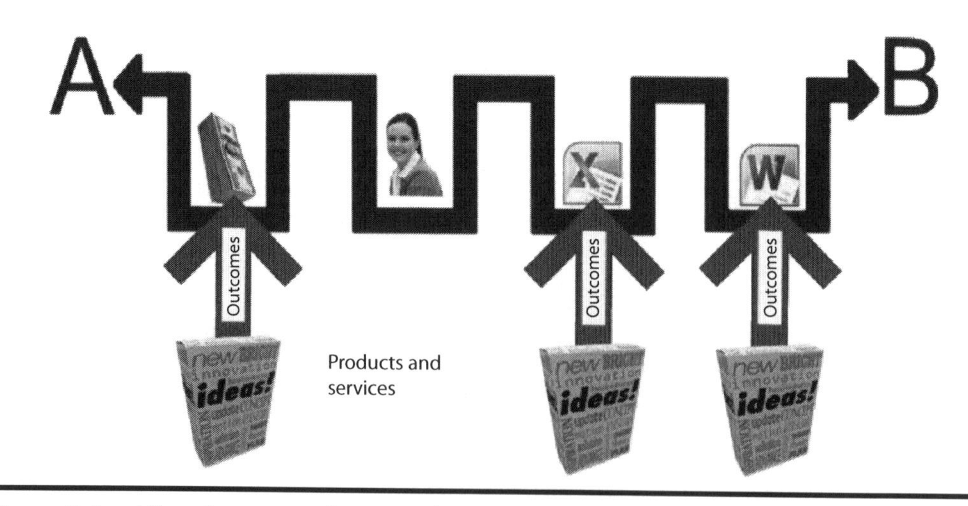


**Figure 2.3 Align the core value creating components or competencies of your product and service to eliminate a customer's waste and successfully enable the delivery of tangible customer outcomes.**

Additionally as a sales organization, it is possible to confirm and prioritize a detailed plan documenting the order in which symptoms can be removed and which symptom will deliver the greatest return or value by eliminating the customers business problem. Using Lean in sales makes it possible to prioritize the delivery of your solution and confirm the financial benefit of the ordered delivery approach. Documenting a planned timeframe for waste removal is what makes your sales proposal personal and enables the customer to recognize the outcome that your solution delivers.

In summary, by looking beyond the customer's problem to the end-to-end process a sales professional is able to identify the root causes of a customer problem. By mapping the process and quantifying the waste in a customer's process a sales professional can identify their products and services that address those 20% of the client's problems (*X*'s) that are creating 80% of their pain (their problem or '*Y*').

## Lean Selling Principle 7: Look Beyond Features, Functions, and Benefits: Capabilities, Outcomes, and Time to Value Are More Important

One of the very first things you learn joining any sales team and being trained in the skills of sales is to break your product or service down into the context of their features, functions, and benefits. This concept is still taught today in many sales training programs. The principle behind it is to break down your product into these three components (feature, function, benefit), and use these components to align your product to a customer need or want.

For example "Did you know Bob that this model car comes with antilock brakes as standard? **(Feature)**" "Should you need to stop suddenly with your family in the car you will be able to push the brake fully to the floor while still being able to steer the car as required" **(Function)**. The benefit to you Bob is that should you ever find yourself in that situation you can continue to steer the car without skidding, keeping control of your vehicle, and ensuring your family's safety **(Benefit)**. The primary intent of using feature, function, and benefit is to align your product or service to the customer and personalize the benefits to the needs or wants of the customer. The example is perfect if we are selling cars to a customer who has told us that safety is of high importance. From a Lean selling perspective, we believe that the feature, function, benefit approach has its place—especially if you are selling intrinsic products and services. However, in today's high technology business world, where you are selling complex products and services, we are endeavoring to define extrinsic value to a customer.

For this reason in Lean selling we focus on **Capabilities**, **Outcomes**, and **Time to Value (TtV)**. In Lean selling, we document a problem and goal statement as soon as possible in working with a customer. Understanding customer business challenges and their business aspirations enables a sales professional to better align 20% or your product and service that will enable 80% of the outcome by eliminating waste and moving the customers' business forward to achieving their goal.

As a sales professional, we still have to build a business case that will substantiate the client's capital investment. It starts by first documenting the capabilities that your products and services will enable. An example of a customer's capability is to "reduce the total number of staff required to approve a loan." More importantly, in Lean selling, we document the outcome that your product and service will create for the customer. In the case of reducing the total number of staff required to complete a loan the outcome will be, "A reduction in operating costs and quicker loan approvals times, and improved accuracy of loan approvals that result in a reduction in the total number of loan defaults." Finally, in Lean Sales we ask the question when (TtV) will the outcome to the customer be enabled? Our answer to this question would be, "our product or service will deliver this outcome in less than 3 months".

In summary, based on an agreed understanding of the customers business problems and goals a Lean Sales professional aligns their product and services based on the following:

1. The Capabilities that your solution will enable.
2. The Outcomes delivered to the customers business as result of your product or service.
3. The Timeframe when your solution will eliminate the problem and deliver the customer outcome (Time to Value)

## Defining Time to Value

While working with sales organizations in relation to their value propositions, you will hear terms like "return on investment," "total cost of ownership," or "total cost of acquisition." There is one word you will hardly if ever hear, "WHEN." By "WHEN?" we mean when will the customer see the net benefits that your product or service will enable. The primary purpose of sales is to confirm to the customer the value of the product or service being sold and how your solution is better than anyone else's in relation to delivering value. Using Lean principles in sales enables your sales organization to quantify the root causes that are creating your customers problem and inhibiting them from achieving their business goals. At this point in time, your customer is sold on the idea. The only question now is "WHEN?"—When can the customer recognize the financial benefit and business outcome that your product or solution enables. The inability to articulate and document exactly when the customer will recognize a financial benefit and business outcome is one to the primary reasons today, that a significant number of sales engagements result in "Do Nothing".

## *Getting to Root Causes Has Never Been So Important!*

Time to Value is as vital to Lean selling as secret herbs and spices are to Colonel Sander's chicken. Working with a customer to mutually agree Time to Value validates the exchange of your product and service for the capital investment in your solution. More specifically, in Lean selling, because we have identified the areas of a customer process that need to be addressed and have confirmed the key wastes. Our sales organization is able to confirm the cost impact of the root causes impacting a customer's process. We are also identifying the key components of the product or service that will eliminate the root causes, creating the customer's problem, and impacting the achievement of a business goal.

By using Lean in sales and getting to this level of detail, it is only now that you can answer the question of "**WHEN?.**" Since your product and service is aligned to the causes that contribute to the clients problem, your value proposition is focused on the components of your product and service that will eliminate the causes of their business problem and more importantly how quickly the process can be improved to deliver net value or a financial return in exchange for a capital outlay by the client. Time to Value documents exactly when financial value will be returned and is illustrated in Figure 2.4; where the sales solutions #1, #2, and #3 are depicted with their respective Time to Value timeframes.

More specifically, though it enables the sales organization to specify which of the root causes has the greatest impact on the customer's business problem, quantifying and prioritizing where to start in delivering a product or service solution to the customer enables two very important differentiators.

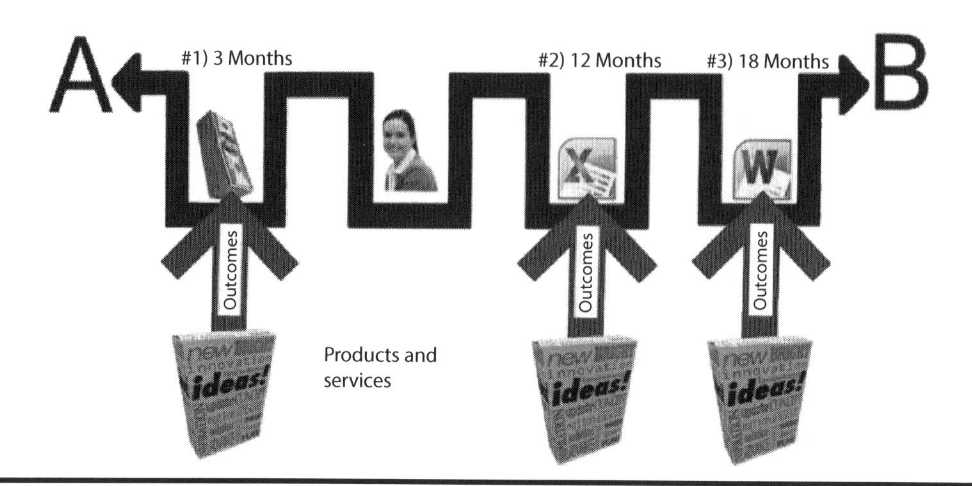


**Figure 2.4 A high-level process map illustrating time to value.**

1. The sales organization specifies the net returns delivered back to your client's business.
2. The sales organization can work with the client to confirm exactly when the root causes of waste can be removed. In the business world today, customers are looking for short-term returns. These are typically expected in less than 6–12 months.

In summary, Time to Value is the "secret sauce" of Lean selling by collaboratively working with a client to confirm "WHEN" the root causes that are creating customer problems or impacting the delivery of a business goal can be removed or contained to deliver a financial return. Additionally, it enables a sales organization to define the the product or service that addresses those 20% of your client's problems that are causing 80% of their pain or business impact, and clients are looking for this value to be provided in the shortest possible time (within 3 to 12 months after purchase).

## *Passing the "So What" Test*

Following the Lean principles, a sales team will work collaboratively with a customer and their internal resources to quantify the process wastes and agree how the capabilities and outcomes of a product and service will deliver value to the customer. Listening to the voice of the customer and ensuring that the customer is at the heart of a sales engagement is key and critical; especially during a capability study. A simple technique that can be used to check the validity of the capabilities and outcomes as defined by the sales team is the "so what?" test. To conduct this test, first prepare and document the capabilities and outcomes and then review them from the point of view of the customer. For example, a capability that the sales team has constructed is to "Reduce the total number of staff required for approving a loan". Acting as the customer, if it is possible for the sales team to respond "so what?" to the capability or outcome then the statement fails the "so what?" test and is rejected back to the sales team to improve it. A capability statement usually fails because it is not refined enough to make it customer specific. Extrinsic value is personal, and customers want capabilities and outcomes that are personal and relevant to them. On the basis of their failing "so what?" test, now the sales team must refine and update their study and capability statement. The capability statement once it has been modified now reads: "Reduce the operating costs of administering loan approvals by 30% or approximately $250,000 per year". As a customer it is much harder to say "so what?" to this capability; primarily because it is more specific and has a financial implication to it. In Lean selling, we are using this "so what?" technique to ensure that the capacities and outcomes are aligned and relevant to the customer. Ultimately, the customer's thoughts and ideas should form an important part of the process of documenting the capabilities and outcomes. However, the more relevant that the sales team can make the documentation for the client, then the more valuable the sales engagement becomes for the client. You know that your capabilities and outcomes are personal and relevant when your customer reads them and says, "Yes, I agree!"

## Challenges Created by the Digital Age—A New Service Model

No matter what product or service you sell, today's business world is highly competitive. Customers are increasingly demanding a lot from their suppliers. Costs for products and services only seem to be heading in one general direction - ever downward. Using Lean principles as part of your everyday engagement with a customer has proven capabilities to provide a competitive advantage, improve close rates, and create true client collaboration. This is typically because of the insight that Lean selling enables in understanding the clients problems and how to fix them. This prompts the question as to why it is important to gain a level of insight into the customer's problems and goals. Why this is more important in today's business engagement as opposed to 5–10 years ago?

For starters, in the last decade the business market has accelerated significantly. There are many factors associated with this velocity but one of the most significant reasons is the advent of the Internet and a dramatic surge in how it is used. With over 2 billion smart phones and tablets in use by consumers, the digital age has created new business markets where "just in time" opportunities await for those businesses that are able to keep pace. It is this pace and alignment to customer demands that is one of the key challenges in the business world today. The advent of social media has created an environment that empowers the consumer to applaud a business for delivering world class customer services. Unfortunately, it can also be used as a super sharp razor to present to the world the shortfalls in your customer services. The ease of access to the Internet through mobile technologies has enabled the consumer to conduct a huge variety of day-to-day functions like paying bills or even buying this book. It also opens new channels for business for to sell to new and existing customers by creating new revenue for those who can keep pace with the change and customer demands. The pace of change in the last 5–10 years has skyrocketed with the customer firmly at the controls demanding ever higher standards of service and mobility.

For businesses small and large they have been left in the wake trying to keep up with an ever fiercely competitive and demanding consumer environment. Additionally, many economies are still recovering from the 2007/2008 financial crisis. At a high level, most customer services models are made up of three basic layers.

## Layers of Customer Services Model

### Layer 1: The Customer

The customer is of course the heart and life blood of the customer service model. The customer will make and break your business. A delighted customer base means a healthy business and no customers equates to zero business. In Lean, we put the voice of the customer at the center of all our projects. Customers typically want services delivered quickly and efficiently and at the lowest possible price. Delighting your customers creates customer loyalty, keeps them coming back for more product and services, and increases their likelihood to recommend your product or service to others.

### *Layer 2: Customer Services and Client Engagement*

The second layer of the customer services model is customer services and engagement. Typically customer facing, these sections either engage directly or indirectly with the end customer, wherein they focus on delivering customer services as part of a product or service. Customer services are (but not limited to) sales or tele-sales sectors, call center staff, and technical support. Client engagement services are departments, such as Internet marketing, dot com e-commerce sales, Internet-based customer care, and up sell. How well customer services or client engagement deal with customers' individual needs and wants has a direct impact on sales, customer satisfaction, and their likelihood to consume more of what you do. Really bad customer services or client engagements can result in the customers telling their immediate friends about the traumas of dealing with the organization. Even worse in today's digital world they can use social media to tell millions of potential customers about the poor service.

### *Layer 3: Business Innovation and Technology Enablement*

The third level of the customer service model is business innovation and technology enablement. This is the back bone of business, enabling the capability for a business to deliver its core business services to a customer. In today's digital age, it is the information technology department who typically deliver the technology and business innovation required to enable customer services and client engagement. Business innovation and technology enablement are arguably the most important group in the customer service model. This is because they enable the delivery of the digital business services in line with customer and competition demands.

## Challenges with the Three-Layer Customer Services Model

The challenge (see Figure 2.5) when looking at the customer service model today is that, first, you have a customer who, thanks to the digital age wants everything delivered bigger, faster, and better. They want the best possible services delivered through a variety of channels (Internet, call center, and face to face). They want to consume those services in a time frame that is convenient to the consumer and they want those services delivered at the lowest possible cost.

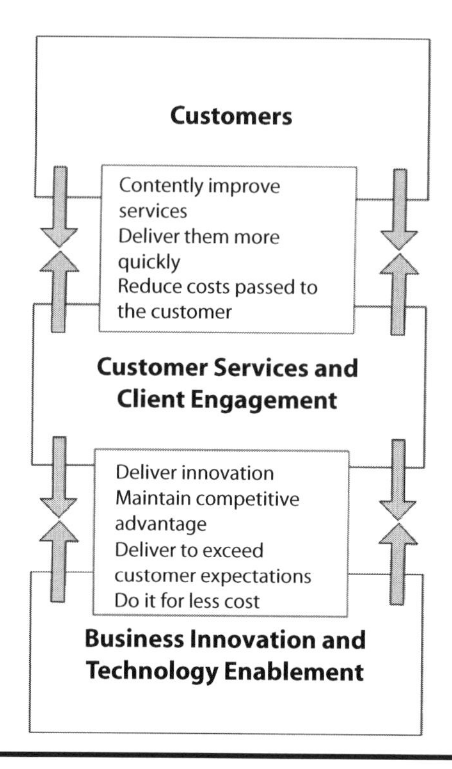


**Figure 2.5 Three layers of a customer services model and the challenges created by the digital age.**

Customer services and client engagement are responsible for exceeding the customer demands while constantly seeking to grow sales, market share, and maintain an edge against the competition. Client engagement is typically dependent on the technology innovation and technology enablement to deliver the capabilities in line with customer, market, and competitive demands. Herein lies the difficulty created by the digital age. The time frames to deliver these customer requirements have reduced significantly driven by digital. So, whereas before it was okay to spend 6–12 months delivering new customer facing products or services, now the customers may require it in less than 6 weeks—or even worse, less than 6 days! A business' ability to be agile and Lean enough to take advantage of "just in time" business opportunities that increase sales, drive customer satisfaction, and improve your competitive edge.

Alternatively your inability to take advantage of "just in time" business opportunities can do just the opposite. Another challenge faced by business today is cost. Managing cost in business is hardly a new idea. But, being agile and Lean at the expense of increased operating costs hardly makes good business sense. To be successful then in the digital age, a business must be both agile and Lean enough to reduce operating costs; while enabling customer services, improving client engagements, exceeding customers' requirements, and maintaining a competitive advantage are all challenges that enterprises face today—both large and small businesses have to face these same daunting challenges.

## *How Can Lean Selling Help Here?—Using Lean Selling for Insight and to Bridge Customer Expectation Gap*

In sales, typically a sales professional will want to meet with and discuss the product and service that is being sold with the broadest cross section of client contacts. In traditional selling, a sales professional will speak with stakeholders typically to gain a more detailed view of the impact that a problem is having on the operation of the business. This view will include insight to the budget for a project, as well as gaining the broadest understanding the customer's problem and the impact it has on their business and their customer service. Typically, it can be very challenging to broaden customer engagement across the three levels of the customer service model. Quite often, customers do not want a sales professional talking to the customer services and client engagement departments. The challenge in a highly competitive sales engagement is improving your capability to gain insight and the details as to exactly how the business problems are impacting customer services engagements. What are the consequences, that ultimately affect the service delivered to the end customer? The more clearly one can quantify the impact of the business problem and its consequences in business terms, the more likely your sales project and business case is to be successful. Figure 2.6 illustrates how process mapping provides insights into problems impacting all layers of the clients customer service model.

Comparing this model with a Lean approach, a Lean practitioner will identify the critical customer requirements (CCRs) as part of a Lean project. Additionally, a Lean project can identify attributes of this project that are critical to quality (CTQ) or critical to customer (CTC). Typically, the CTQs of a project are the internal CTQ parameters that relate to the needs and wants of the customer. In a project documenting the CTC requirements a project would define what is most important to the end customer or consumer of the service. Another measure a Lean practitioner might identify in a project is the cost of poor quality (COPQ). The COPQ is an important measure because it typically measures the cost involved in working around the gap between what the customer expects and the actual quality of the product and service being delivered. It can also be used to measure the cost of lost

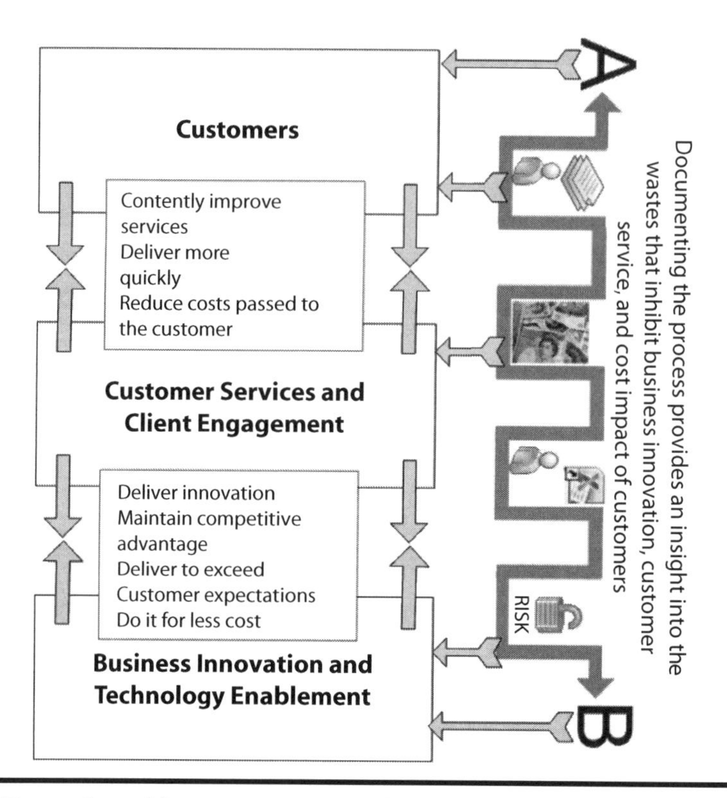


**Figure 2.6 Illustration of how process mapping provides insights into problems impacting all layers of the client's customer service model.**

opportunity (e.g., releasing a new web-based product to the end consumer 4 days late, or reallocation of resources within a company to bring a project back on track).

Given the challenges of doing business in the digital age how does this effect sales organization's client engagement and its alignment to the three layer customer services model? How does Lean selling help to overcome engagement obstacles in the digital age?

The first key advantage is that Lean selling focuses on breaking the problem and goal down to the process level. It quickly maps the process end-to-end in relation to the problem. Typically, this is achieved by mapping the process and documenting it down to a Lean waste level. As this is done, insights into the impacts that the waste is having on all three levels of the customer services models will begin to become clear. In fact, it is often an outcome of Lean selling projects that the client will actually arrange meetings for you to meet key contacts across the organization, rather than having to struggle to arrange them yourself.

The second key advantage of using Lean selling principles in projects is that Lean selling has been created to be accurate and agile. In order to keep up with the pace of change created by the modern business world and the digital age, it is important that decisions about change are made quickly and accurately. After all, failure to keep pace with the changing needs and wants of a customer can often be fatal in business.

The third key advantage of using Lean selling principles in projects is that the measurement of CCRs, CTCs, CTQs, and COPQ can provide quantitative, and financial impact information relative to the client's customer service model. Measuring the impact of waste as it relates to a process enables a sales organization to build a business case that is personal to the client.

Finally, many of the wastes that Lean selling identifies can have cascading effects on a business. A cascade effect is the unidentified or unmeasured consequences of a problem. Problems often impact multiple segments of service delivery, multiple departments of a business, and ultimately the customer. Identifying and removing cascade effect problems will streamline customer service models, reduce operating expense, and significantly improve the customer's ability to respond to "just in time" opportunities.

## Chapter 3

# The Lean Sales "Funnel" Framework Explained

> No problem can ever be solved from the same level of consciousness that created it.
>
> **Albert Einstein**

In Lean selling, we want to spend a majority of our time understanding a client's business problem and unique situation before we can offer a solution that is right for them. This approach is the only way to provide extrinsic value to the client that is personal and unique. The Einstein quotation at the beginning of this chapter is quite relevant as a thought starter for this topic; as Lean selling requires a profound change in thinking. Some sellers may measure their own success by counting how many sales they closed over the past year, how much revenue they provided their company by way of their deals, and of course how much money they earned in the way of their sales commissions. All of these are important measures of success for sure; however, what is more important is that the products and services that the sales professional delivers are providing the business value promised to their client. While most sales professionals understand this critically important principle, the traditional methods they use for conducting a sales engagement do not always guarantee that this principle holds true. The Lean selling approach brings the principle of delivering client value to reality by way of its approach to the client engagement, and the Lean selling methods are a unique and powerful way to ensure that a seller is delivering *value*.

Fully understanding business challenges and specific problems is the key to Lean selling success! How is this done? How can a sales professional identify a customer's problem with enough understanding and insight that the client will buy into it? Not only do our clients need to believe that we understand their business challenges and unique situation well enough to support our recommendations, they also need to tell others in their organization that our solution is the right solution to fix their problems. General managers, CFO's, vice presidents, and presidents all need to agree that our solution addresses the specific and unique challenges of their businesses, and they need data lead proof that product or service being offered will have the business impact that is promised. So once again, how is this done? Lean selling is a methodology that encompasses the end to end sales cycle, so let us start at the beginning.

In Chapter 1, we talked about the traditional "sales funnel" as the overarching framework for engaging a client throughout the end to end sales cycle. In Figure 3.1, the Lean selling sales funnel is depicted. Let us first start with the market in which our products and services serve to find an appropriate market opportunity for Lean selling. Identifying the appropriate client to call on is an important first step with the Lean approach to sales. While there is no guarantee that we will identify the right sales opportunity 100% of the time, the Lean tools provide a highly efficient and effective way to target account opportunities; where the Lean selling approach will likely work. This approach does not preclude a sales professional from calling on any and every client, but it will help to prioritize which ones should be called on first. After all, targeting the right customers early helps to ensure the most efficient use if a sales professional's valuable time.

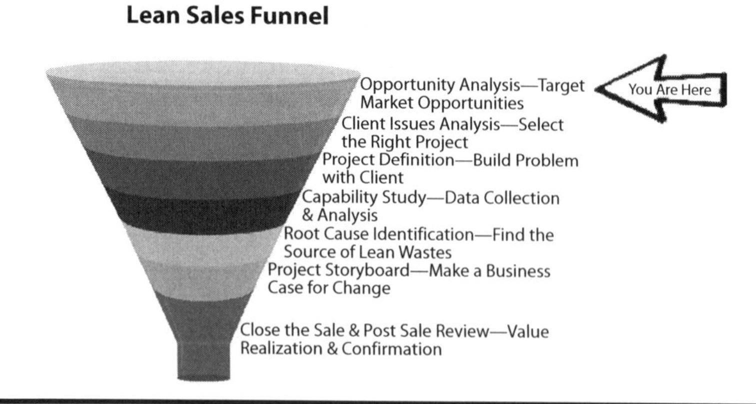


**Figure 3.1 The Lean Sales Funnel outlining the stages of a typical Lean selling client engagement.**

## Opportunity Analysis

The Lean selling approach for targeting market opportunities begins with a technique that is called *opportunity analysis*. This approach is best applied with the support of an extended sales team. Most people can appreciate the power of team-based decision making as being superior to decisions made by a single individual. The perspective of an entire client facing team is much broader and more insightful than that of any single individual; including the sales leader. While the sales leader typically leads a sales engagement, strategy, and actions, it is important that the engagement be coordinated and facilitated to ensure input from a broader team. Good teaming ensures when working through the market analysis activities that all members have an equal voice in the process. The process itself is designed to be very collaborative and objective. Objective team-based decisions minimize the potential for personal opinions and biases that sway the decision making process. Typically, in an hour meeting with the sales leader and their entire team, an effective and useful market *opportunity analysis* can be performed.

The technique is carried out by use of an objective criteria-based selection tool. Criteria-based decision making is one of the fundamental tenets of Lean selling and helps to provide some of that very important "science" to sales planning and client engagements. Decisions based on objective criteria and facts are far superior to those made by the subjective opinion of any one individual. A team's criteria-based decision ensures that two key outcomes are realized: (1) decisions are objective and well thought out, and (2) decisions are made collaboratively, leveraging the inputs and insights of the entire sales team. Even subject matter experts can have biases when it comes to making decisions. For example, a sales professional can believe he or she knows all there is to know about a certain market or group of clients, yet they can easily overlook information that is critical for making a sound decision. A team-based decision making approach provides the perspective of the entire sales team and results in superior outcomes. The criteria and an illustrative example of a sales *opportunity analysis* template are shown in Table 3.1.

Using sales opportunity analysis, a sales professional can review the various client engagements and sales opportunities that they are considering and list them in the first column of the template. The first factor to consider when evaluating potential selling opportunities is the "importance" of the opportunity to the customer. Starting with this criterion is in keeping with the principle of placing the customer's needs first, so starting this step evaluates to what degree is the customer impacted by

**Table 3.1 A Market Opportunity Analysis Template for Lean Sales**

| *Market Opportunity* | *Project Importance to Customer 9-High 3-Med 1-Low* | *Current Relationship 5 - Very Good 4 - Good 3 - Fair 2 - Poor 1 - Very Poor* | *Importance to Business 5 - >$1M 4 - >$.7M - $1M 3 - >$.4M to $.7M 2 - >$.2M to .$.4M 1 - $.1M to $.2M* | *Resources to Close 1-High 3-Med 9-Low* | *Probability of Success 90% - Very High 75% - High 50% - Moderate 25% - Low 10% - Very Low* | *Time to Close 1 - 1 Year + 2 - 9 to 12 Months 3 - 6 to 9 Months 4 - 3 to 6 Months 5 - 1 to 3 Months* | *Leverage Other Opportunities 9-High 3-Med 1-Low* | *Overall Rating* | *% of Total* |
|---|---|---|---|---|---|---|---|---|---|
| The Gadget Shop: XYZ Data Xchange 2000 | 9-High | 5 - Very Good | 3 - $500,000 | 1 - High | 75% - High | 1-3 Months - 5 | 9-High | 4556 | 63% |
| Bilbox E Shopping: XYZ Data Xchange 3000 | 3-Med | 3 - Fair | 2 - $250,000 | 9 - Low | 90% - Very High | 6-9 Months - 3 | 3-Med | 1312 | 18% |
| ABC Online: XYZ Data Xchange 4000 | 9-High | 2- Poor | 4 - $800,000 | 9 - Low | 25% - Low | 1-3 Months - 5 | 1 - Low | 810 | 11% |
| Gilbore Online Shopping: XYZ Data Xchange 5000 | 9-High | 1 - Very Poor | 3 - $500,000 | 1 - High | 50% - Moderate | 6-9 Months - 3 | 9-High | 365 | 5% |
| Matrov Network: XYZ Data Xchange 1500 | 1-Low | 4- Good | 1 - $100,000 | 3 - Medium | 90% - Very High | 9-12 Months - 2 | 9-High | 194 | 3% |
| **Total** | | | | | | | | **7237** | **100%** |

the successful completion of this sales project? Specifically, how does it improve its financials and align with its business strategies? Alternatively, some traditional target market opportunity analysis techniques may start with the amount of revenue it can generate for the seller's company. This traditional approach begins this critically important step of account targeting and immediately introduces a serious bias; by placing the needs of the seller ahead of the needs of the client.

## *Criteria 1: Importance to Customer*

For each opportunity, the "importance to customer" is rated using a high, medium, or low rating scale, which is then converted to a numerical score with a high rating receiving the highest score and a low receiving the lowest. The scoring is assigned a score of 9 for a "high" rating, a score of 3 for a "medium" rating, and a score of 1 for a "low" rating. It is important to note that these scores are proportional to one another. In other words, a "high" rating receives three times the score of a "medium" rating, which is three times the score for a "low" importance rating. These ratings help to clearly differentiate between a "low" and "high" importance opportunity from a customer perspective. Of course, this criterion (like the other criteria, as well) reflects the sales team's perspective of the project's importance to the customer. Other Lean selling methods will validate whether or not the team's "hypothesis" is valid. At this point in the sales cycle, the sales team perspective is an excellent starting point and will lead to better client engagement decisions. Table 3.2 illustrates this criterion and the rating for each potential selling opportunity in our simple example.

**Table 3.2 Example of the "Importance to the Customer" Criteria and Ratings for Potential Customers**

| *Potential Client and Sales Project* | *Project Importance to Customer*[a] |
|---|---|
| The Gadget Shop: XYZ Data Xchange 2000 | 9—High |
| Bilbox E Shopping: XYZ Data Xchange 3000 | 3—Medium |
| Matrov Network: XYZ Data Xchange 1500 | 1—Low |
| ABC Online: XYZ Data Xchange 4000 | 9—High |
| Gilbore Online Shopping: XYZ Data Xchange 5000 | 9—High |

[a] 9—High, 3—Med, 1—Low.

## Criteria 2: Current Customer Relationship

The "current customer relationship" is also evaluated and this five scale rating ranges from very poor to very good, where the numerical scores used here range from 1 to 5, respectively. What is the overall relationship with the sales organization and the client? When prioritizing market opportunities, the status of the current business-to-business relationship is another important factor, and one that requires objectivity and honesty by the entire sales team when evaluating this relationship. It does not do the sales professional any good to overestimate the quality of the relationship. Having a realistic view of the true quality of the relationship will be critical to the sales team later on, as an engagement strategy is developed for the respective clients. While even a "poor" business relationship can be turned around with the right sales team and a compelling business opportunity, it is always helpful to know the relationship status when approaching any sales opportunity. Of course, a comprehensive strategy would be required to turn around a poor relationship, and that can be the focus of a subsequent sales team discussion. At this point in the Lean selling process, an honest estimate of the business-to-business relationship begins to set realistic expectations about the likelihood of a client to buy from your company. All things being equal, a "good" business relationship will probably result in closing a deal long before another sales opportunity where there is a "poor" relationship with the client, so this criterion is also very useful when evaluating multiple sale opportunities. An example of the "current relationship" criteria and rating can be seen in Table 3.3.

**Table 3.3 An Example of the "Current Relationship" Criteria and Ratings for Multiple Sales Opportunities**

| *Potential Client and Sales Project* | *Current Customer Relationship* |
|---|---|
| The Gadget Shop: XYZ Data Xchange 2000 | 5—Very good |
| Bilbox E Shopping: XYZ Data Xchange 3000 | 3—Fair |
| Matrov Network: XYZ Data Xchange 1500 | 4—Good |
| ABC Online: XYZ Data Xchange 4000 | 2—Poor |
| Gilbore Online Shopping: XYZ Data Xchange 5000 | 1—Very poor |

[a] 5—Very good, 4—Good, 3—Fair, 2—Poor, 1—Very poor.

## *Criteria 3: Importance to the Sales Organization's Business*

The next evaluation criterion is the "importance to the sales organization's business" for each opportunity being considered. Here, the sales team determines to what degree the company is impacted by the successful completion of this project? The reality of the business world is that everyone is in business to make money. While it is not the only factor considered when evaluating multiple sales opportunities, it can help the seller's business to objectively determine the value of the opportunity from a strategic perspective (and it indirectly justifies the level of sales support that is appropriated for a given opportunity).

While there are other factors to be considered in terms of the importance of a given client opportunity, this factor focuses on the level of business it will generate, or specifically the size of the sales opportunity in terms of revenue potential. These ratings are constructed relative to the level of business that each opportunity could produce in terms of revenue to the seller's business. Of course, the level of revenue created from a sales opportunity will vary from industry to industry, so the opportunity analysis template can be customized for this field, as needed. Other measures of a sales project's importance will be evaluated independently using other criteria as to keep all relevant factors of the sales *opportunity analysis* in proper balance. Table 3.4 shows this criterion and its ratings for the sales opportunities under consideration by the sales team.

## *Criteria 4: Resources to Close*

A sales professional and their company's management must clearly understand in advance of embarking on a sales lead how much resource is anticipated to close a sale. While there is much unknown about most sales opportunities,

**Table 3.4 An Example of the "Importance to the Seller's Business" for a Sales Project[a]**

| *Potential Client and Sales Project* | *Importance to the Seller's Business* |
|---|---|
| The Gadget Shop: XYZ Data Xchange 2000 | $500,000 |
| Bilbox E Shopping: XYZ Data Xchange 3000 | $250,000 |
| Matrov Network: XYZ Data Xchange 1500 | $100,000 |
| ABC Online: XYZ Data Xchange 4000 | $800,000 |
| Gilbore Online Shopping: XYZ Data Xchange 5000 | $600,000 |

[a] 5—> $1M, 4—$.7M to $1M, 3—$.4M to $.7M, 2—$.2M to $.4M, 1—$.1M to $.2M

and Lean selling is very much about a mutual client and sales organization discovery process, a sales professional and sales team must anticipate to the best of their ability the amount of time, effort, and resource required to justify value and close a sale. After all, if a sale will take 10 sales persons time and 18 months to close, maybe it is not worth pursuing in comparison to the other opportunities being considered. Once again, a "high," "medium," or "low" rating is used to estimate the resources needed to bring a sales opportunity to fruition. The sales team must keep in mind that these are relative ratings, so it is useful to identify the sales opportunity the team thinks will be the *most* resource intensive and give that the "high" rating, then rate the other sales opportunities relative to it. As with the other ratings, they are replaced with a numerical score so that it can be used in subsequent calculations.

Much of this particular rating is based on experience; which is why it is so important for a team-based approach for this evaluation. Like all team-based activities, the more these disciplines are adopted and practiced, then the more accurate, relevant, and useful they are to the actual client engagement experience. For sure, gaining a broad perspective of the resources needed to qualify and deliver a sale is key and critical for an accurate assessment. Everyone is prone to biases, and it is easy for one member of the team to underestimate the effort required by another team member. For example, the sales leader may not realize the amount of time and effort required from the technical sales team, so having the technical team involved in the decision-making process is vital to realizing an accurate outcome. Hearing from the entire team and reaching consensus in relation to their insightful estimate of the resources required to close the sale is the best approach for this criterion. Table 3.5 provides an example of the "resources to close" criterion and its ratings for each of the sales opportunities that the team is evaluating.

**Table 3.5 The "Resources to Close" Criterion and Ratings for the Various Sales Opportunities Considered**

| *Potential Client and Sales Project* | *Resources to Close*[a] |
|---|---|
| The Gadget Shop: XYZ Data Xchange 2000 | 1—High |
| Bilbox E Shopping: XYZ Data Xchange 3000 | 9—Low |
| Matrov Network: XYZ Data Xchange 1500 | 3—Medium |
| ABC Online: XYZ Data Xchange 4000 | 9—Low |
| Gilbore Online Shopping: XYZ Data Xchange 5000 | 1—High |

[a] 1—High, 3—Med, 9—Low.

## *Criteria 5: Estimated Probability of Success*

Our next selling opportunity analysis criterion is the estimated probability of success for the sales project. Here, the team evaluates likelihood of a successful close to the opportunity and compares it in relation to other sales projects that will require the sales team's engagement. These probabilities are represented as a percentage, which can be thought of as the "confidence level" of the sales team in closing the sale. For example, a "very high" confidence level in closing the sale would receive a probability of success of 90%. This percentage is used as a de-rating factor for the overall score. As an example, a "probability of success" rating of 50% would result in a reduction of the overall score by half. While experienced sales professionals perform this kind of assessment instinctively, this criterion-based approach makes what is otherwise a "personal" decision, and replaces it with a visible and evident thought process and one that is now confirmed by the entire sales team.

This criterion, as well as the entire opportunity analysis template, can also be shared with the sales management team as the rationale for the sales team's intended "sales engagement" strategy. Properly determining which sales opportunity that the team invests its valuable time in and deciding when to engage with a client can set the stage for the team's activities for the next several months to follow (depending, of course, on the length of the sales cycle). This entire opportunity analysis approach is referred to as a "go slow, to go fast" process. Time is invested up front to identify and plan the sales call strategy, which ultimately results in saving time for the entire team by engaging where it makes the most sense for the client, as well as for the sale team. Table 3.6 shows an illustration of the "probability of success" criteria and ratings for each market opportunity.

## *Criteria 6: Time to Close*

Next, the sales team estimates the length of time required to confirm value to the customer and when they expect to close each sales opportunity. The estimated time to close will, of course, vary depending on the industry, so the time frames in the template can be customized. In Table 3.7, the "time to close" estimates are shown along with the numerical ratings for our simple illustration. In principle, the shorter time to close receives a higher numerical rating than a longer time to close. This assessment allows the sales team

**Table 3.6 The "Probability of Success" Criterion and Ratings**

| *Potential Client and Sales Project* | *Probability of Success*[a] |
|---|---|
| The Gadget Shop: XYZ Data Xchange 2000 | 75%—High |
| Bilbox E Shopping: XYZ Data Xchange 3000 | 90%—Very high |
| Matrov Network: XYZ Data Xchange 1500 | 90%—Very high |
| ABC Online: XYZ Data Xchange 4000 | 25%—Low |
| Gilbore Online Shopping: XYZ Data Xchange 5000 | 50%—Moderate |

[a] 90%—Very high, 75%—High, 50%—Moderate, 25%—Low, 10%—Very Low.

**Table 3.7 Example of the "Time to Close" Criterion and Its Ratings for the Multiple Sales Opportunities**

| *Potential Client and Sales Project* | *Time to Close*[a] |
|---|---|
| The Gadget Shop: XYZ Data Xchange 2000 | 1–3 Months—5 |
| Bilbox E Shopping: YZ Data Xchange 3000 | 6–9 Months—3 |
| Matrov Network: XYZ Data Xchange 1500 | 9–12 Months—2 |
| ABC Online: XYZ Data Xchange 4000 | 1–3 Months—5 |
| Gilbore Online Shopping: XYZ Data Xchange 5000 | 6–9 Months—3 |

[a] 1—Over 1 Year, 2—9 to 12 Months, 3—6 to 9 Months, 4—3 to 6 Months, 5—1 to 3 Months.

to consider the investment of its valuable time (duration of the sales engagement) along with the elapsed calendar time, as a factor to consider when evaluating market opportunities.

## *Criteria 7: Leverage For Other Opportunities*

Last, the sales team determines the ability to leverage this particular client opportunity for additional future business. In other words, how will other projects in the client's organization become affected or influenced by the successful completion of this project? For example, the business opportunity at hand may provide the client with an important platform upon which future capabilities can be built. It is important to note that completing this evaluation is quite appropriate and critical, as identifying the potential strategic importance for a client opportunity helps to create a long-term relationship where the sales professional becomes a trusted consultant for the client. As future business challenges arise within the client's organization, the client will be the one to contact the sales team and not vice versa. Table 3.8 illustrates the criteria and ratings for "Leverage For Other Sales Opportunities"

## Consolidating the Ratings across the Seven Criteria

Finally, the sales team can objectively evaluate the many opportunities that exist amongst its clients by discussing the "overall rating" results. A numerical total can be evaluated to determine where the best market opportunities exist (Table 3.9). The most attractive opportunities should be reflected by higher overall scores relative to the other opportunities. It is critically important to note that this selection template itself does not make the final sales project selection for the sales team; but rather, it supports the decision making process. The sales team must reach consensus on which client opportunity or opportunities it pursue first. In other words, this decision support tool provides the sales team with objective information to help them make better decisions.

These seven criteria can be evaluated during one meeting amongst the key individuals within a sales team. The more this method is followed, the easier and quicker the process flows; which results in a realistic view of the company's sales opportunities landscape. To be effective, however, there are three guiding principles for the team to follow when using this method. These principles are as follows:

**Table 3.8 The "Leverage for Other Opportunities" Criterion and Ratings for the Sales Opportunities**

| *Potential Client and Sales Project* | *Leverage for Other Opportunities*[a] |
|---|---|
| The Gadget Shop: XYZ Data Xchange 2000 | 9—High |
| Bilbox E Shopping: XYZ Data Xchange 3000 | 3—Medium |
| Matrov Network: XYZ Data Xchange 1500 | 9—High |
| ABC Online: XYZ Data Xchange 4000 | 1—Low |
| Gilbore Online Shopping: XYZ Data Xchange 5000 | 9—High |

[a] 9—High, 3—Med, 1—Low.

**Table 3.9 The Overall Rating Fields of the Opportunity Analysis Template**

| *Potential Client and Sales Project* | *Overall Rating* | *% of Total* |
|---|---|---|
| The Gadget Shop: XYZ Data Xchange 2000 | 1519 | 56 |
| Bilbox E Shopping: XYZ Data Xchange 3000 | 656 | 24 |
| Matrov Network: XYZ Data Xchange 1500 | 194 | 7 |
| ABC Online: XYZ Data Xchange 4000 | 203 | 8 |
| Gilbore Online Shopping: XYZ Data Xchange 5000 | 122 | 5 |
| **Total** | **7237** | **100%** |

1. Everyone's open and honest input is required. Every team member has equal status on the team and its contributions to the discussion are invaluable. A good sales team leader needs to set the tone for the team meeting. He or she must create a safe environment where everyone feels compelled to contribute to discussions and decisions.
2. The ratings are relative to one another, so the team should strive for a range of ratings across its many opportunities (for example, if all opportunities are rated as "very high importance" then, in effect nothing is of high importance since they are all weighted to be of equal importance.
3. The team must reach "consensus" on each of its ratings. Consensus means that each team member can support the rating agreed upon by themselves and all other team members. Reaching consensus takes time; however, it provides the sellers with a broad perspective of the market opportunities and yields a decision that the entire sales team will support.

NOTE: If the team is uncertain about any of its criteria or ratings associated with a specific customer opportunity, then specific engagement actions are agreed upon by the sales team to obtain the missing information and confirm it with the customer.

# Chapter 4

# Combining the Art of Selling with the Science of Lean—Getting Started

> If I had an hour to solve a problem I'd spend 55 minutes thinking about the problem and 5 minutes thinking about solutions.
>
> **Albert Einstein**

Now that the sales team has agreed and prioritized the client projects which will be the primary focus for this sales engagement, they now need to begin planning around how they will engage with the client on that particular business opportunity. In this chapter, our Lean selling method proceeds to the initial client communications that begins with the first sales engagement with a client.

One of the guiding principles of Lean selling is that every piece of documentation produced during a sales cycle should be shared with the customer. It is, after all, due to the fact that we share something of value first that creates an environment of true collaboration between a sales organization and the customer (the principle of giving). The giving often starts by building a problem or goal statement based on insights found on the Internet or in the corporation's annual reports. Taking the time from the first meeting and every meeting there after to attend with something well thought out and personal immediately creates a transparency that shows the customer your intent to truly understand their needs. Even if the document that is built is not completely accurate or if it does not perfectly represent the problems that the customer is challenged with today, this is okay! It is okay because you have shown the customer your intent to understand their business, and your ability to think independently. Ultimately, this approach gives a sales professional an opportunity to question and update the document with the customer so that it accurately represents their business needs and wants omit 'or problems or goals'.

Sales organizations use words like "trusted advisor" very loosely, and very rarely do they have the methodology or make the commitment of time to develop a real "trusted advisor" relationship. Lean selling is the methodology that can make this phrase a reality, and using the Lean selling practices, a professional sales person can significantly reduce the time taken to establish a truly collaborative client relationship. Most clients are pleasantly surprised to learn that the sales professional is not going to try to "push" a solution upon client, but rather they desire to "pull" relevant information from client and their organizations to better understand their unique business issues. It is this ability to "pull" the relevant information relating to a specific customer problem and goal that will enable a sales organization to build a business case for their products or services. This business case must be relevant and specific to that customer and their unique needs. In Lean, it is an important fundamental principle to "pull" value from the client. The same holds true in sales. Pulling the right information at the right time is vital to providing the client with the value that they truly need. The first "pull signal" in Lean selling is the definition of the client's unique problem and goal.

Before the client's problem and goal can be specifically defined, a sales professional must first bound the scope of the problem. See the Lean selling funnel diagram in Figure 4.1 as we enter this next stage of the sales cycle. In formal problem solving terms, this approach is referred to as identifying the "point of cause." The point of cause is not the same as getting to root cause. The point of cause is the last observable sign, or symptom, of a customer's problem. In order to validate the client's root cause, quite a bit more work using Lean selling techniques is required. A critical first step in working toward root cause analysis is to properly scope the problem, or business issue, from the client's perspective. An effective tool to assist in determining the point of cause of a client's specific business challenge is to develop an opportunity, or issues, analysis 2 × 2 matrix (Figure 4.2). This matrix helps a sales professional to agree on the magnitude and boundary areas of business problems with the client. Building this picture will assist the sales team to understand the relevance of the customer's business problems.

**Figure 4.1 The Lean sales funnel highlighting the client issues analysis stage.**

The naming convention, 2 × 2, originates from the fact that the matrix displays business issues or improvement opportunities against two criteria (business benefit and time to value) and each client issue is evaluated at two levels (high and low levels) for each criterion; hence the term 2 × 2. In this case, issues are depicted by the 2 × 2 matrix, *with* each client issue

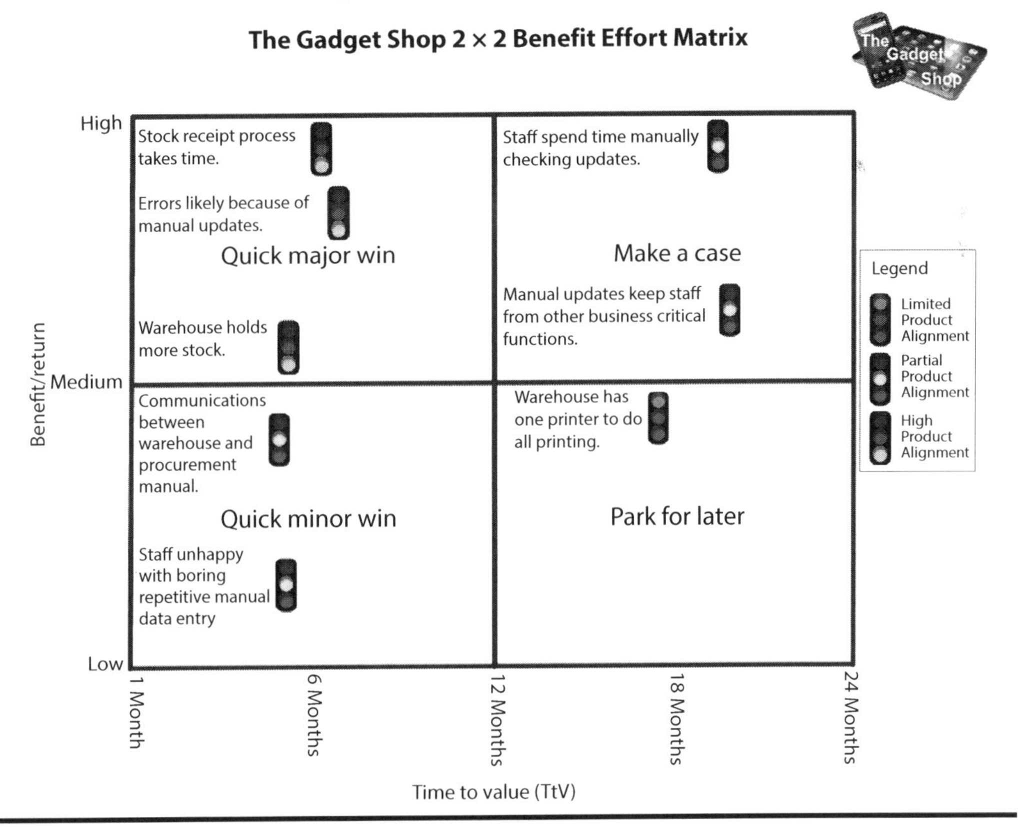


**Figure 4.2 Issues analysis 2 × 2 matrix for The Gadget Shop.**

being evaluated against the aforementioned criteria. The criteria represented on the *Y*-axis of the matrix is the business benefit, or value, that each of the client's business issues would return if that issue was to be resolved. For this criterion, there is no proposed solution at this point in the sales cycle (since the root causes of these problems are not fully understood); only the business issue itself is represented in the matrix. The business benefit is of course a projection of the returned value that the seller and client believe will be the "relative" value realized by solving each opportunity.

The point of determining the "relative" business value is important to emphasize here. Again, the 2 × 2 matrix uses a qualitative "High" or "Low" rating for evaluating the benefit realized by resolving each business issue. The sales professional and the client agree upon a numeric rating for each issue (or business opportunity) on a scale of 1 through 5; where 1 is "very low" and 5 is a "very high" business benefit. The use of the numeric rating system allows the sales team to compare one business challenge to another. While it is a qualitative evaluation, this approach enables the sales professional to quantify the value of resolving a number of the customer's business issues. Comparing the projected values of resolving these business issues or opportunities is necessary, but it is not sufficient in terms of deciding which one to take on first. The amount of time that it is expected to take to realize this business benefit is another important criterion to be used to evaluate the client's many business issues.

The same relative rating approach is followed for the "time to value" criterion, which is represented by the *X*-axis of the 2 × 2 matrix. Here the business issues are evaluated by the team and client based on the amount of time it will take to realize the business benefit once the business problem is resolved. Of course, this is an estimate based on the sales professionals and client's best guess; however, this information is very useful in terms of prioritizing opportunities for the sales team, and also for the client's organization. While a numeric 1–5 rating system can be used here as well, it is more useful to use actual time estimates that the sales professional believes can resolve the business challenge for the client. For example, the *X*-axis can range from 1 month up to 24 months (as illustrated in Figure 4.1). Of course, this range can be customized depending on the magnitude of the client's specific business challenges. Once again, the "time to value" estimates are best guesses made by the sales professional and they are agreed upon by the client. Once the business benefit and time to value are estimated for each of the client's business challenges, then the sales professional and client can have an insightful discussion around what challenge makes the most sense to begin working on first.

It is often useful to use a third selection criteria to the 2 × 2 matrix. The third criteria commonly used during this stage of the sales engagement is "alignment of the issue to the sales professionals products and services"; which is depicted in Figure 4.2 with red, yellow or green stop lights. A "green" stop light for example illustrates a client's business issue where the sales team believes they have an offering to address it. This criterion is useful in helping the sales team focus on those client issues that they can help to address.

This issues and opportunity analysis exercise, while it is seemingly a simple activity, truly changes the dynamic between the sales professional and client. The traditional dynamic of a sales professional "pushing" solutions to the client will quickly shift to a collaborative problem solving approach; where solutions are ultimately "pulled" by the client. They are "pulled" because the customer has collaborated with the sales team and understands the quantified value as it relates to them personally. In fact, clients can often be quite surprised by a sales professional working collaboratively, using quantitative information to "pull" them toward a solution and the valuable business outcomes that are enabled. It is common to find the client "pulling" more and more information than is actually needed at the time. A sales professional who experiences this "pull" for the first time will find it quite shocking, because he or she almost immediately moves from a sales engagement where the customer shares next to nothing, to an engagement where a client willingly shares everything!

In our previous chapters, it has been explained and emphasized that "value" is personal for each and every client. A personalized approach to defining value is therefore required in order to offer a solution that is meaningful to a client. Now that the seller and client agree on the appropriate business challenge or challenges to begin working, the sales professional can begin a deeper dive into a specific challenge by defining a problem statement that accurately reflects the customer's specific business challenge. Let us reference our Lean sales funnel, and notice that we have progressed to the next stage of the funnel; which is our initial communications and deliverable in the form of building a problem statement with the client (see Figure 4.3).

Among his many famous contributions, Albert Einstein was quoted as saying (in so many words) that "a problem well-defined is more than half solved." In other words, spend the majority of your time to understand a problem fully and in-depth, before moving to a solution. Human nature often encourages us to rush to a solution before we fully understand a problem

**Figure 4.3 The Lean sales funnel highlighting the problem statement development stage.**

"and it cause." One of mankind's greatest strengths is our ability to solve problems. Humans have put a man on the moon, cured numerous diseases and have solved countless problems that plagued our world. However, strengths can often become weaknesses if they are not kept in check. We humans are such great problem solvers that far too often we start developing a solution to a problem, before we take sufficient time to fully understand the problem itself. In the world of sales, when we rush too quickly to a solution without gaining sufficient understanding of our client's problem, we offer solutions that miss the mark and often result in lost sales. If we are lucky enough to close the deal without our fully understanding the client's needs, there is the risk that we provide a solution that does not totally fix the client's problem and they are left feeling let down. Typically, this scenario results in a loss of trust and a diminished chance of securing future business.

In Lean selling, the *Pareto Principle* is an important part of our sales engagements. Most everyone understands the Pareto Principle as the *80/20 Rule*. From a problem solving perspective, a sales professional's role is to quantify the 20% of the client's problems that is causing 80% of their pain. For sales professionals this principle means that they should spend the vast majority of their time understanding, documenting, and verifying the client's problems, and then invest the remaining time aligning their product or service to eliminate that problem and satisfy the client's specific business needs. This approach actually shortens the sales cycle because the seller achieves greater "buy-in" from the client (and other key decision makers) since the proposal truly addresses the unique needs of the client's business. Depending on the product and service that you sell, activities like proof of concepts, pilots, and other justification-type activities become required less by the customer and may even stop becoming a client requirement all together. This happens because by working with quantitative information that is directly related to the customer's problem and accurately aligning the 20% of your product portfolio to eliminate 80% of the customer's problems often eliminates the need for a proof of concept.

The first point of engagement with a client relative to a prospective sales opportunity is defining the problem statement. In Lean selling, if there is *no problem statement*, then there is *no sales cycle*. In fact, without a problem statement, the sales cycle can often lack sales focus and direction; resulting in a series of exchanges that never leads to a solution for the client or a sale for the sales team. The problem statement is foundational, not only to the Lean selling method, but critical to any sales approach. Without a clearly defined problem and goal, it can become quite difficult in complex sales engagements to keep the entire sales team focused on the right sales engagements at the right time. The lack of a documented problem can elongate the sales project, hence making it very susceptible to a lack of focus and inconsistent direction. The net result can be a higher than average sales failure rate and increased sales engagement wastes and inefficiencies as a result of working on sales activities that never progress to a closed sale. Additionally, not having a clear focus on exactly what the customer's problem is can result in a sales organization proposing a solution that the customer does not recognize as valuable to its business and to their unique circumstance. This misalignment happens because the client and sales team may all truly believe they are working toward the same end, however, without a well-defined problem and goal statement; often times the individuals involved are working to solve slightly different problems.

In competitive sales situations (which most sales are; as multiple companies often compete for a client's valuable business), the client may even allow the sales team to proceed down this blind path in the spirit of letting the seller bring forward the offering that they believe is the best for the client. After all, the sales team understands their offerings much better than the client, so the client assumes the team knows what they are doing. Of course, this approach results in a proposed solution that does not meet the expectations of anyone, and in particular, it misses the specific needs of the client. At the end of the day, any sales engagement that does not result in a sale is a form of Lean waste and a real cost to your business as a sales organization. It is therefore vital that all sales engagements are given the greatest possible chance to close.

Creating an effective problem statement is not as easy as it might seem. While there is an element of "art" involved in developing an effective problem statement, there are a few useful guidelines that should be followed. The acceptance criteria for an effective problem statement are described as follows:

1. Clearly describes the current state or current situation
2. Clearly describes the desired state or desired situation
3. Explains the business impact of not being at the desired state
4. Clearly, completely, and concisely articulates the customer's current state problem
5. Explains the implications that the problems are having on the customer's business operations, which are typically categorized in the context of Lean wastes
6. Quantifies the financial impact that the problem is having on the customer's business

The problem should be specific and observable in terms of clearly describing the current state. A specific and observable problem is key as it is one that can be "checked off" the list when solved. Vague or ambiguous problem statements leave everyone guessing as to whether or not the problem was ever solved. Being specific means getting beyond vague and nebulous problem statement such as the following example from our fictitious on-line retailer, The Gadget Shop:

> *The Gadget Shop is losing sales as a result of its manual updates to its central stock and price file!*

A more specific problem statement that meets all the acceptance criteria might read similar to the following: This problem statement leaves out many important details; like how are manual updates creating this situation and how much sales are lost as a result?

### *The Problem Statement*

> *The Gadget Shop is an online gadget sales retailer. To make products available for sale the company updates a central stock and price file on a weekly basis. The update of the central file is manual (Motion Waste) and takes up to 8 hours per week to complete. The update of the central stock and price file results in it taking up to*

*6 days to make stock available for sale (Waiting Waste). Last year 416 errors were identified as a result of manual data entry (Defect Waste). Recent growth in the popularity of The Gadget Shop online the company has seen increased customer complaints and cancellation of orders (Defect Waste). This problem is currently costing The Gadget Shop annually $460,000 in lost sales, including operating inefficiencies due to motion and defect wastes, as well as reduced profits due to incorrect pricing updates.*

If the problem that The Gadget Shop is having gets resolved through some course of deliberate action by the company, they then can "check off" that problem from the numerous others on their list of problems and priorities to be resolved. Also, note that there is a desired state indicated in the new problem statement. The company desires to remove the requirement to manually update the central stock and price file. A clear "gap" of $460,000 between the current and desired state can also be discerned. Last, notice there is a business impact statement that is described in the detailed problem statement. Not only is the problem costing $460,000, but it is impacting Gadget customers and costing the company sales orders. Another impact statement within the problem statement is that there were 416 data entry errors identified and a higher customer order cancellation rate in recent months. These impact statements should be a compelling reason for the business executives and those working within the business to solve the problem.

An effective problem statement should answer the "what" and "so what" about a client's unique situation. Specifically, what is the problem they are experiencing and what is the impact of that problem? In other words, how motivated is The Gadget Shop to solve this particular problem? While it is far too early in the Lean selling cycle to talk about the root cause or root causes of this problem, an effective problem statement provides the client with the proper motivation to work closely with the sales professional to solve the problem. Once the problem is validated and signed off by the client, it now sets the stage for a deeper dive into the client's business in search of root causes.

Before a sales professional and client begin their quest to tackle the root causes that are creating the client's problem, they must first develop an effective goal statement to go hand-in-hand with the client's problem statement. In Lean selling, the problem and goal statement are referred to as "book ends." You cannot have one without the other, as they both frame the current situation and describe what the client's business will look like once the problem is solved. A problem statement should never be presented to the client without its counterpart—the goal statement. The problem and goal describe the beginning and end state of the sales cycle. Of course, the sales professional is looking for the assignable root causes of this particular problem so they can offer a solution by way of a product or service offering that addresses these causes and achieves the client's goal. This approach makes the sales process very personal to the client, and as was noted in Chapter 1, extrinsic value is always personal. The only way to deliver extrinsic value is to identify a client's specific problem and its causes and by demonstrating that your product or service is uniquely equipped to remedy that problem.

When constructing a goal statement, much like the problem statement, there are guidelines that help a seller construct an effective one. First of all, when developing a goal statement the sales professional should always reflect on the mnemonic S-M-A-R-T. **SMART** goals are those that meet the following criteria:

**S—Specific:** Similar to the problem, the goal needs to be observable so it can be "checked off" when it is achieved. A sales professional can only confirm that they have delivered on a goal that is specific; whereas it is never clear whether or not a vague goal is ever actually achieved.

**M—Measurable:** The ability for a client and sales professional to objectively assess progress against, and ultimately the achievement of, the goal requires that it to be measurable. A measurable goal ensures that the sales professional and client can objectively determine the degree to which the sales solutions addresses the client's problem.

**A—Achievable:** The goal should be aggressive yet achievable. Only the sales team and client can judge achievability. Avoid goals that are overly aggressive, such as "achieve 100% customer satisfaction, as perfection is an ongoing pursuit but often never achieved or sustained indefinitely.

**R—Relevant:** The goal should be meaningful to the business. The support needed by the sales team will only be garnered if the client's business is motivated to solve the problem. Of course, the client's input into and validation of the goal statement is key and critical to Lean selling "by ensuring the project's goal is relevant to the client."

**T—Time Bound:** The "time to value" concept is a critical element of the goal statement as well. This aspect of the goal statement is the time it takes for the product or service offering to deliver the projected value to the client's business. The time to value proposition is the key to differentiating the Lean sales professional's product from other sellers' products.

The following is an example of a goal statement for The Gadget Shop:

### *The Goal Statement*

*The Gadget Shop will improve its customer service* ***(critical to customer requirement)*** *as an online retailer by improving the accuracy of its central stock and price file. Achieving this goal will result in stock being available for sale immediately upon receipt into the warehouse. Finally, achieving this goal will result in an annual revenue increase and operating cost savings. Our commitment is to achieve this goal by the end of The Gadget Shop's fiscal year.*

In this goal statement you may have noticed that the goal can be even more specific and measurable. Creating objective goal statements is where the development of balanced success measures can be very useful. It is also extremely effective when a sales professional includes these success measures and associates them with the goal statement, such as sub-text to the goal. When defining success measures, a balanced scorecard approach is quite helpful (Kaplan and Norton, 1992). The balanced scorecard approach ensures that the project's success is looked at holistically and takes on a broad view of the client's business performance. The four components, or metrics, of the balanced scorecard are customer, financial, process, and people performance measurements. A balanced approach to measuring a sales project's success ensures that a project's goals are not too narrowly defined. For example, If a sales engagement *only* focuses on a financial return, the proposed solution could actually be detrimental to people working with the business process we are trying to fix for example. The balance scorecard is described further in Table 4.1.

From a Lean selling perspective, the sales team uses the Lean sales balanced scorecard in a slightly different manner than that of the traditional balanced scorecard approach. The sales team uses the scorecard to put themselves in the place of the client when asking key questions. For example, the traditional balanced scorecard approach would be to ask "How can we improve the way *our* business appears to *our* customers." The Lean selling approach asks a slightly different question. The Lean sales team asks, "How can our products and services improve the way our *client's* business appears to *their* customers," which is an important shift in perspective. This approach puts the sales team in the shoes of the client's and takes on their perspective in terms of satisfying the needs of the *client's* market and their customer base. While this point may seems subtle, it can change the

**Table 4.1 The Lean Selling Balanced Scorecard**

| *Scorecard Components* | *Key Question?* | *Measurements (Examples)* |
|---|---|---|
| **Customer Satisfaction** | *How are The Gadget Shop customers affected by the achievement of this goal?* | Customer satisfaction, retention, lower complaints/increased compliments, response time, market share |
| **Financial Excellence** | *How are The Gadget Shop shareholders, operating costs, and/or its annual sales impacted by achieving the goal?* | Sales growth, profitability, return on equity, improved cash flow |
| **Internal Process Excellence** | *To satisfy The Gadget Shop customer requirements, which processes must our client do well at, and how will process performance be measured?* | Cycle time reduction, reduced, errors/defects lower, operating costs, increases in innovations, improved operating efficiencies |
| **Employee Learning and Growth** | *To improve The Gadget Shop processes, what skills and abilities must our employees develop?* | Employee retention, morale, training, employee engagement, skills adoption |

conversation insofar as the questions the sales professional asks the client, and is critically important in terms of convincing the client that the seller's goals are aligned with the client's goals. Additionally, like everything in Lean selling once a position has been documented by the sales professional and the sales team who are selling the product and service, it is fed back to the customer to gather their feedback and gain their support. Gaining customer feedback is vital to test the assumptions for accuracy and alignment with the customer's own opinions and views. Getting this crucial client information is how *value* is personalized and how insight into *extrinsic value* is revealed.

The financial aspect of the balanced scorecard follows a similar approach. Here, the key question of the sales professional is "How can our offerings help the client's business look better in the eyes of its shareholders." Solutions that help the client to improve its financial position by increasing its top line (revenue), lower operating costs that improve its bottom line (profits) and/or improving its quote to cash cycle time (cash flow) are measured by this particular balanced scorecard measurement. Examples of financial balanced scorecard are described in Table 4.1. Often times, this is the *only* measurement in which the sales professional focuses, ignoring other aspects of a balanced scorecard (customer satisfaction, internal process efficiencies, and people skills). While financial impact claims can be critical to closing a sale, to focus solely on financial benefits overlooks other important aspects of the clients business, such as its customers, its internal business processes, and its employees.

Next, let us describe the internal business processes measurement of the balanced scorecard. Here is where the Lean sales professional has a distinct advantage over the *traditional seller*. For internal business processes, the question asked by the sales professional is "What are the important business process "performance measures" in which the client must excel in order to satisfy the expectations of its customers and shareholders?" This book will outline the Lean selling methodology in much more detail, and for now, it will suffice to describe the Lean selling method as providing the sales team with a deeper understanding of the client's internal processes; so that a solution can be offered that addresses the specific and unique problems that exist within those processes. This Lean approach is fundamentally the secret to sales success! While specific techniques for performing this analysis will be described further in subsequent chapters, a few examples of a client's internal business process performance measurements include lower process cycle times, reduced error rates, improved resource utilization, and other key process performance indicators impacting operating efficiencies and/or effectiveness.

The fourth component of the Lean selling balanced scorecard takes the perspective of improving the client's employees learning and growth. Here the key question becomes, "How will your products and services improve the client's business processes and assist its employees to develop skills and capabilities that are critical to its business success?" Not unlike other "people" measurements, these metrics are often the most difficult to tangibly measure, although they are arguably the most important of all the balanced scorecard components. In keeping with the principle of introducing more scientific management to the field of sales, we will once again call on one of the greatest scientific minds of all time, Albert Einstein, who is quoted as saying, "Not everything that counts can be counted, and not everything that can be counted counts." When considering the "people" success measurement, these are the ones that count the most for businesses, although they are never easy to count. "Soft" measurements, such as people and organizational culture related metrics are certainly the most challenging to quantify and document, but are well worth the effort since they are the arguably the most important measures of business success.

A key Lean principle is that people are an organization's *only* appreciating asset. While the client's building, equipment, tools, and IT infrastructure will all depreciate over time, the client's employees must appreciate for its business to be successful. This principle is a simple, yet profound concept that offers a distinct advantage for the sales professional, who considers how his or her offerings can have a favorable impact on employees' learning and growth. Clearly, by documenting these "people" success measures as a part of the sales engagement goal statement, it differentiates Lean selling goals from traditional selling goal statements. Some examples of employee learning and growth measurements include number of employees trained, number new skills attained (and applied), and the number of new innovations generated by employees as a result of these new skills.

The following is an example of a goal statement (revisited) along with the Lean sales balanced scorecard success measures and metrics (Table 4.2).

### *Goal Statement (Revisited) and Balanced Success Measures*

*The Gadget Shop will improve its customer service* ***(critical to customer requirement)*** *as an online retailer by improving the accuracy of its central stock and price file. Achieving this goal will result in stock being available for sale immediately upon receipt into the warehouse. Finally, achieving this goal will result in an annual revenue increase and operating cost savings. Our commitment is to achieve this goal by the end of The Gadget Shop's fiscal year.*

Table 4.2 illustrates how the balanced scorecard success measures help add clarity and specificity to The Gadget Shop goal statement. When discussing the balanced scorecard approach to identifying success measures, let us also mention the important concept of "leading" and "lagging" indicators. The term indicator here is synonymous with success measurements or metrics. Of the four balanced scorecard components, the financial and customer measurements are considered to be the *lagging* indicators and the process and people components are considered the *leading* indicators. A leading indicator can be considered a predictor or early warning system for the lagging indicators. In other words, if an organization is working to improve its key process and people indicators, then it is lagging indicators of its key financial and customer measurements will show improvement as well; albeit at some later point in time. The key point here for the sales

**Table 4.2 The Lean Sales Balanced Scorecard for The Gadget Shop**

| *Scorecard Component* | *Success Measurement* |
|---|---|
| **Financial** | Eliminate the operating costs and cash flow impacts associated with carrying 15% extra stock, and resulting in an annual saving $460,000 per annum. |
| **Customer** | Increase customer satisfaction due to stock availability and best pricing policy. Have inventory for an order in stock 98.5% of the time when a customer visits our web site. Reduce orders cancelled per month due to stock unavailability by 50%. |
| **Process** | Eliminate motion and defect wastes as a result of manual updates to stock and pricing records. Eliminate up to 8 hours a week spent manually updating the price and stock file; as well as additional work by the warehouse staff to manage stock and make it available for sale. Free up procurement staff to find amazing suppliers at the best credit terms. |
| **People** | Minimize the employee talent waste and enable staff to use role-based expertise to deliver highest levels of customer service. All Gadget employees to be trained and certified in Lean methods. |

professional is to never overlook the *leading* indicators, although the business owners focus on the lagging indicators. In terms of confirming the value delivered by your product or service, by working closely with the client to measure those leading indicators, you can make the necessary course corrections when needed to ensure that the customer and financial success measures (lagging indicators) meet or exceed their targets. As an illustration, a *leading* indicator for The Gadget Shop is the time taken from receipt of stock in the warehouse to updating the inventory and price files (a process indicator). The team could also ensure that there is less mundane steps for the inventory teams at The Gadget Shop (Leading indicator: People), thereby reducing their frustration and aligning them to value added steps.

By streamlining this process and maintaining the time to do this step in minutes can have a positive effect on the *lagging* indicators of financial and customer excellence. Based on the above scenario, having the accurate inventory and price lists ensures that the cycle time for the order to reach the customer will also be on target (lagging indicator: Customer satisfaction) and thereby, affects The Gadget Shop's profitability (lagging indicator: financial excellence) positively.

Identifying one or two key performance metrics for each balanced scorecard component is sufficient for establishing balanced success measures. Selecting the appropriate leading and lagging indicators is critical to a company's ability to effectively monitor its progression toward business success, which in Lean selling terms is the predefined "goal" of the sales project. With Lean selling, a sales professional becomes quite skilled at identifying those indicators that are fundamental to improving a client's business by way of its unique problem, specific goal, and ultimately your proposed solution to your client. This book will outline the Lean selling method as a powerful means for delivering a unique and effective client solution, and one that beats the competition.

## Reference

R.S. Kaplan and D.P. Norton. (1992). The balanced scorecard: Measures that drive performance. *Harvard Business Review,* 70(1): 71–79.

*Chapter 5*

# Client Capability Study and Identifying the Eight Deadly Forms of Lean Waste

> Look deep into nature, and then you will understand everything better.
>
> **Albert Einstein**

The Einstein quote, "Look deep into nature, and then you will understand everything better," implies that a deeper understanding is required to gain sufficient knowledge in order to successfully solve a problem. While a sales professional is not expected to be an expert in the laws of physics and other underlying principles of nature, the Einstein statement can and does apply to the world of sales. Similar to Einstein's request to look deep into nature, by continuously qualifying and breaking down a sales engagement into a series of phases, a sales professional is able to identify the key components within a client's process that contributes to the cause, or causes, of its unique problem. The Lean selling approach is one that takes a process perspective in order to identify the unique process performance issues that allow the sales team to customize a solution that is meaningful to the client. This process-oriented approach can be extremely powerful in the world of sales, as client's business processes are the common threads that can unite information technology, finance, and the business operations teams that are otherwise stand-alone functions within the client's organization. Figure 5.1 illustrates the Lean sales funnel and the progress we have made since the first step in this journey.

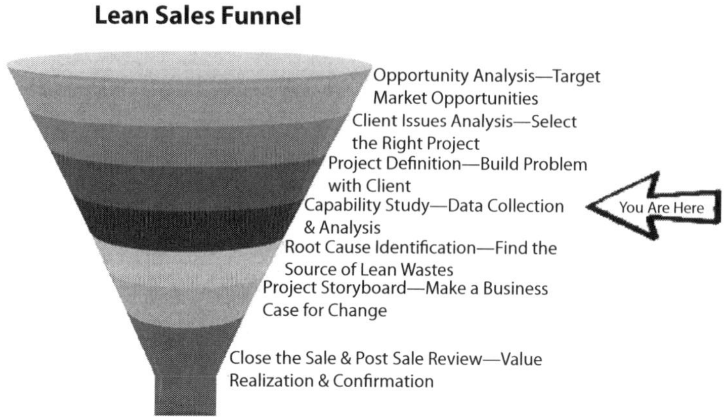

**Figure 5.1 Lean sales funnel highlighting the capability study.**

A traditional sales engagement will typically engage and work with just one of the business functions within an organization to progress the sales cycle and ultimately close a sale. As a sales professional, it is important that the art of sales is used to convince the customer of the importance of a particular product or service in improving a certain aspect of their business. Depending on the product or service sold twenty years ago, when selling, if you could convince one person within the clients organization of your product's worth that was probably enough to close a sale. Today, a professional sales person must convince multiple people in the customer's organization that their product will deliver significant business value. Depending upon the products or services that you sell, your client engagement may need to convince roles like the IT manager and chief information officer (CIO), as well as the operations and plant management, and let's not forget the finance manager and probably even the chief finance officer (CFO). Suffice to say, the list of people who have influence, if not control, over the decision to purchase a product or service is probably pretty long. The budget for your product may very well be in competition for something else equally important but entirely different than what you are proposing. With fixed budgets and limited investment dollars, the decision to spend is becoming even more difficult for today's business world. It would not be unheard of to lose a sale because the staff's coffee machine is considered a more important investment than your product; which may seem absurd but it really does happen, and illustrates just how tight operating budgets have become.

A sales professional will typically rely on one key individual or a small number of sponsors within the organization to help champion their product offerings. These sponsors are vital to help sell the value of the sales proposal to other key decision makers, such as operations and finance. This leaves the success of your sales proposal in the hands of the keys sponsors and your sales success (or not) resting with their ability persuade their peers that your proposal is sound and worth investing in. In contrast, the Lean selling approach identifies the specific areas within the client's business processes that will be greatly improved as a result of the proposed sale's solution. The communicated solution and the outcomes align to the client's process as a common language such that stakeholder business functions can relate and understand how your solution value relates to them personally. This makes the acceptance of the proposal more likely. Additionally because a Lean engagement improves a process owned by multiple business functions, it increases the likelihood that during the sales engagement you will be given the opportunity to meet more of the business function stakeholders and gain their input. Why does this situation take place? It happens because, as a Lean sales professional, you are always working on a project that is real, relevant, and valuable to multiple key stakeholders within the client's business. The Lean selling method provides a consistent and standardized approach for the client, such that a after a few engagements a client knows what to expect. They can begin to rely on the Lean approach to document and understand the company's problems and ultimately know how their unique challenges can be addressed by way of your product and service offerings.

The Lean sales professional quickly becomes a trusted advisor to their clients and are warmly welcomed when calling on them. In terms of sales effectiveness, the Lean selling methodology is able to align your sales strategy to only those aspects of the client's business that are valuable to them or problematic to their business; this result is a much more efficient sales engagement. The solution is unique and personal to the client in that it addresses the root cause of their problem and delivers extrinsic value; hence, making every sales engagement, and every sales proposal (*Lean storyboard* described further in Chapter 9) extremely valuable to a sales organization and completely relevant to the customer.

Lean selling's root cause investigation and verification are the foundation of providing the client with "extrinsic value." As we have already described in our previous chapters, extrinsic value is the "holy grail" of sales, as it is unique and personal to every client, and once it is discovered it truly differentiates a Lean sales professional from all other traditional sellers. It is important to note, that Lean selling is a "discovery" process. At the onset of the sales engagement, the sales professional really does not know exactly how their products and services will solve the client's problem until they uncover its root cause. Identifying the root cause (or causes) with the client, and by providing them with a solution that addresses those specific causes makes the proposal unique and personal from a client's perspective. Determining the extrinsic value that a product or service provides versus the competition is a key differentiator of Lean selling over traditional sales methods, and results in a dramatically higher close rate.

Assuming that the Lean sales professional starts with a client's problem and goal as described in Chapter 2, the next step is to perform a client capability study. The purpose of the capability study is to work with the client to identify the root cause or causes of the client's specific problem. This is the point in the Lean sales cycle where the Lean principles are employed by the sales team and client. A good starting point with the client is to prepare a supplier-inputs-process-outputs-customer (SIPOC [pronounced "*psy-pock*"]) diagram with your client. The Lean and Lean Six Sigma practitioner will recognize the SIPOC diagram as a useful tool that is applied early in their improvement effort, and is an important project management technique for scoping the project and identifying key stakeholders to involve in the project work. As a Lean seller you do not have to be an experienced Lean practitioner or certified Black Belt in order to develop a SIPOC diagram with your client. Spending about an hour interviewing your client and a few members from the client team should result in sufficient information to create a useful SIPOC diagram. Like all other sales methods, knowing what to ask your client, when to ask it, and knowing who can best answer specific critical questions is the key to sales success. This chapter will outline the SIPOC diagram and how it should be used during the sales cycle as the foundation for your project's success. The following will give you the insights for successfully developing one with your client.

The letters S-I-P-O-C in the term SIPOC diagram is actually an acronym or mnemonic that stands for Supplier-Inputs-Process-Outputs-Customer. The SIPOC diagram is a high-level illustration of the client's end-to-end process under investigation. In addition to scoping the project (or client's problem) and identifying key stakeholders to include in the project, the SIPOC activity starts the sales professional (and client) down the path of "$Y$" as a function of "$x$" thinking [$Y = f(x)$]. As we have described in an earlier chapter, the "$Y$" is the output or outcome from a client's process (or a specific measurement of that outcome). For example, our customer—The Gadget Shop—is an online retailer that sells various gadgets at discounted prices to thousands of customers around the globe. In addition to a low price, The Gadget

Shop promises customers a quick dispatch and supply of all of their online gadgets. In fact, many Gadget customers even request next day delivery, which offers a profitable shipping premium for the company. Suffice to say, having product available for their customers at all times is a key business objective for The Gadget Shop. The "*Y*" in this scenario is of course related to the business outcome from The Gadget Shop's online store, and more specifically, it can be the customer's satisfaction with their online shopping experience. Another possible "*Y*" in this scenario is the cycle time taken to receipt new stock that the customer has ordered and deliver these goods to the customer (i.e., customer serviceability time). The time it takes for the customer to return unsatisfactory gadgets and receive a credit could be another "*Y*." See the SIPOC diagram illustrated in Figure 5.2 that shows a completed end-to-end stocking process for The Gadget Shop. The Lean sales professional and client will most likely focus on one particular "*Y*", but it is The Lean sales professional and client who ultimately decide on one particular that will make for the most meaningful sales project.

| S<br>Suppliers | I<br>Inputs | P<br>Process | O<br>Outputs | C<br>Customer |
|---|---|---|---|---|
| Gadget Shop procurement | Warehouse replenishment signal | Place order with supplier | Purchase order, confirmation and delivery commitment | Gadget Shop supplier |
| Gadget Shop procurement | Delivery updated in accounts system | Received goods into warehouse | Warehouse inventory system update | Gadget Shop warehouse staff |
| Gadget Shop warehouse staff | Inventory location transaction | Place goods in "Not For Sale" area of warehouse | Dispatch notes given to procurement | Gadget Shop procurement |
| Gadget Shop procurement | Combined dispatch Purchase orders | Dispatch notes and purchase orders combined | Documents sorted in receipt date order | Gadget Shop procurement |
| Gadget Shop procurement | Price and stock updated for received stock | Update central stock and price file | Stock release advise for review | Gadget Shop procurement |
| Gadget Shop procurement | Updates checked | Check and authorize system updates | Stock release advise Delivered to warehouse | Gadget Shop warehouse staff |
| Gadget Shop warehouse staff | Warehouse staff move stock | Move stock to be "Ready for Dispatch" area of warehouse | Dispatch notes printed | Gadget Shop warehouse staff |
| Gadget Shop warehouse staff | Back orders and daily orders pick list | Pick orders | Accounting system updated | Gadget Shop warehouse staff |
| Gadget Shop warehouse staff | Order ship list and packaging | Dispatch orders to customer | Customer order and invoice | Gadget Shop customer |

**Measureable Characteristics**

| Input Measures | Process Measures | Outputs Measures |
|---|---|---|
| Days orders waiting to be received<br>Inventory location errors<br>Time to update stock file<br>Time to check stock file<br>Number of order on back order<br>Number of stock outs | Cycle time<br>Days waiting in "Not for sale" area<br>Motion time<br>Motion distance<br>Central stock and price errors<br>Time spent correcting errors | Number of stock and order errors<br>Time to update inventory<br>Errors in stock release advise<br>Time to generate dispatch notes<br>Customer complaints<br>Customer orders returned |

**Figure 5.2 An illustration of The Gadget Shop's online inventory management process using a SIPOC diagram.**

It is important to point out that a SIPOC diagram is not intended for process analysis but rather as a tool to visualize the process steps and, begin to understand the extent, or scope, of the customer's problem. Additionally, a sales professional can begin to understand where the process is failing and who are the various important process stakeholders. Last, the SIPOC is a good starting point for identifying the important measureable characteristics within the process. Remember, the process output *Y* is a function of the process *x*'s, so identifying those *x*'s and *Y*'s begins the discussion of cause and effect [$Y = f(x)$] relative to the client's problem. We will describe other techniques for a deeper analysis into the client's process, and for now, we will focus on the SIPOC as it is intended to be used as a tool for initial insight into the customer's problems.

Prior to starting the development of a SIPOC diagram, the sales professional and client should agree upon a project "*Y*" of interest. In our illustration, the project "*Y*" is the cycle time taken to receipt new stock that the customer has ordered and deliver the goods to a customer. Further to the importance of this project "*Y*," the owners of The Gadget Shop have seen an increase in order cancellations and customer complaints due to long delivery times. In fact, to contain this problem the company has started holding extra stock, which has a negative impact on the company's operating costs and cash flow. Not having enough stock on hand may be a result of manually updating a central stock and price file; which could be the primary reason why the company is seeing an increase in customer dissatisfaction and cancelled orders. The action of holding extra stock may not actually be helping to remedy The Gadget Shop's problem. Gaining insight into The Gadget Shop's process and understanding how well it works will help determine the business impact of our project "*Y*," which we will agree upon as a next step, but first we need to complete our SIPOC diagram. Once the SIPOC is completed, the sales professional will review it with the client's key stakeholders to validate, and then reach consensus on the project "*Y*" to be further investigated. The key point here is that deciding on the project "*Y*" will make the conversation around understanding the process that delivers that specific outcome much, much easier for the sales professional. Once the "*Y*" is determined, the client and sales team can begin a deeper discussion around the "*P*" in SIPOC, which is the "Process" that delivers the project "*Y*." A Lean sales professional understands that a quality process delivers a quality outcome ("*Y*"), and it is their fervent belief in this principle and adherence to the Lean selling methodology that makes that client a believer as well.

When creating the SIPOC diagram itself, a sales professional should start with the client's description of their end-to-end process at a high level.

Typically, 5–7 high-level process steps are all that is required to describe an end-to-end process. Limiting the number of process steps forces you and your client to define the process at a very high level. Again, the intent here is not to perform a detailed process analysis, but rather to gain a fundamental understanding of the key operations performed within the client's process, and it is also useful for gaining some insight into who (what functional areas) performs these high level operations. For example, it is useful to know that the warehouse staff will start The Gadget Shop process once orders are receipted into the warehouse. We now know that the warehouse staff are important stakeholders in this process. Additionally, the procurement team is important stakeholders too. To be successful in closing a sale to The Gadget Shop, it would be vital to our sales cycle to involve both departments and help them understand how their work will be improved if we fix the current Gadget Shop process. A sales professional working collaboratively with a customer using these Lean selling techniques has much greater insight into a customer's problems. Specifically, "Who" in the company must we collaborate with and "How" does the problem affects these key stakeholders (as seen in our SIPOC diagram), hence enabling a much clearer and more detailed view of where the problem is actually occurring. Gaining insights and involvement from everyone affected by a problematic process can only make a sales professional's and customer's relationship stronger, and it ensures that your business case is being built upon a foundation formed by facts (the science of selling) rather than subjective hearsay and conjecture.

The other benefit of creating a SIPOC diagram is that it bounds a few areas within the process where root causes, or critical "*x*'s," can be found. Remembering that the "*x*" is a cause or causes (multiple "*x*'s") relating to The Gadget Shops increased customer complaints and order cancellations. For example, an "*x*" in The Gadget Shop process is the fact that the company's systems are reliant on the manual updating of the stock levels and central price file. Errors created in the price and stock level file can be considered a process "*x*." While this is not necessarily a root cause of The Gadget Shop's problem, it bounds an area in the client's process for deeper analysis. The next step for the sales team and client is to perform that deeper dive around the processes relating to stock ordering, product availability, and customer delivery. To that end, the team will develop a value stream map (VSM) which will help the client "see the wastes," or inefficiencies, that exist within the process. Remember, we only want to fix those parts of a process that are broken, and the other areas of a process that are working well will be left alone.

A VSM is a very effective technique that has been used by Lean and Lean Six Sigma experts for years, and is foundational to any process improvement effort. As the name implies, the VSM looks at an end-to-end process to see how *value* is flowing from supplier to customer. Value is defined as something that a customer is willing to pay for. For a sales professional, finding the specific reason that will make a customer pay for your product or service is the very reason that the sales role exists so finding the value creating activities within a client's process will become second nature for a Lean sales professional. Furthermore, "Value," from a customer perspective, should flow smoothly across the entire value stream with minimal delays and inefficiencies. The VSM is an excellent way to visualize how well value actually flows throughout a process, and provides a good view of the eight deadly forms of Lean wastes that might exist within the process. Figure 5.3 illustrates these destructive forms of Lean wastes. They are appropriately called "waste" because they represent the inefficient and ineffective activities within the process that delay the delivery of client value. Anything less than the optimal use of the valuable resources of equipment, materials, people, space, and

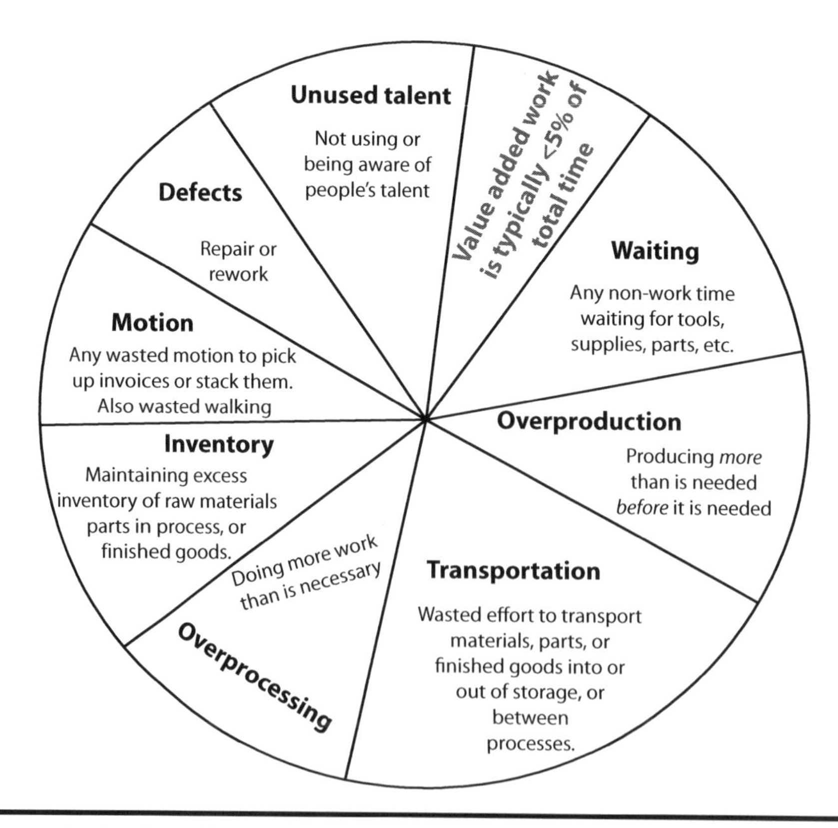


**Figure 5.3 A pie chart illustrating the eight deadly forms of Lean waste.**

time is considered a Lean waste. A typical process—one that has not been optimized using Lean methods—can exhibit 90% or more of its deliverable's (it's products or services) time spent in these nonvalue creating activities.

## Lean Wastes

Identifying and eliminating Lean wastes are the foundation of Lean process improvement and the same is true for Lean selling. Identifying the client's Lean wastes is vitally important because this becomes a common language that the sales team and their customer can use to effectively describe the symptoms that are causing the customer's problem. More importantly for the sales team and the customer, Lean wastes can be quantified in terms of their cost impact to the client's business. Understanding the costs associated with a waste enables the sales professional to build a business case that is real and extrinsically relevant to the customer such that it their support for a product purchase. Lean wastes once explained to the client become the primary focus and context of the client engagement. It is an exceedingly simple approach, yet amazingly powerful. No one wants to have a process full of Lean wastes and your client is no exception.

Another important aspect of Lean wastes to consider, as a general rule, is that customers today have probably already undertaken the easy projects to improve their efficiencies and reduce operating. In other words, they have already harvested the low hanging fruit. What remains in relation to business improvement opportunities typically, are the tougher less visible projects. Helping the client to "see" these different forms of wastes within their own processes is an important next step for business improvement. One of the best ways that a sales organization can be proactive in their engagements is to help their customers identify the extrinsic value associated with the improvement of their business efficiencies and reducing their costs. When a sales team is successful in delivering this value proposition then they are going to be sought after as a key business partner. The Lean selling methodology offers a unique approach for identifying extrinsic value by eliminating a client's Lean wastes.

## Explanation of the Eight Lean Wastes

### *Waiting*

Waiting waste is a waste that occurs in most processes. Of course the amount of waiting waste will vary from process to process. As an example, a worker who is waiting 2 hours for a report to arrive before they can perform a task is a form of waiting waste. In the case of The Gadget Shop, waiting for the warehouse staff to receipt goods into the warehouse, and then waiting for the procurement department to update the central stock and price file are both examples of waiting wastes in the inventory management process. As a customer, you would not be willing to pay for time spent waiting as it provides no value to you. The impact of this waste can be measured in terms of cycle time and what it costs The Gadget Shop in terms of increased operating costs.

## Overproduction

Overproduction waste is defined as producing more than is needed before it is needed. For example, if The Gadget Shop was to package for shipping several orders of their best-selling gadget before actually receiving a customer order, it would constitute as an overproduction waste. These orders would wait for an actual order to be placed and may wait for a long time (now waiting waste is incurred). In fact, some gadgets may never ship, so they will get unpacked and returned to stock (motion and transportation waste). At first glance, building more than is required might seem valuable to The Gadget Shop since they are trying to anticipate their customers' needs, but unless it is immediately consumed by a customer, then it is actually a Lean waste. Overproduction is one of the deadliest forms of Lean waste in that it can result in the recreation of other wastes as well.

## Transportation

The Lean waste of transportation is the wasted time and effort to transport or move a product from one location to another. In the case of The Gadget Shop, the warehouse staff moves stock to a "not for sale" area of the warehouse until it can be released for sale. The effort of moving the stock to and from this area is a form of transportation waste. The effort and time expended by the warehouse staff to perform this activity can be measured in terms of cycle time and increased operating (labor) costs. Additionally, the cost of allocating space in the warehouse for the "not for sale" area is a cost impact, as The Gadget Shop has a monthly lease cost for this warehouse space.

## Overprocessing

Overprocessing (sometimes called Extra Processing) waste involves doing more work than is necessary. For example, The Gadget Shop takes 8 hours to update the central stock and price file. This task, if automated, can be done in a matter of seconds. Overprocessing for The Gadget Shop delays the release of orders to their customers and increases their operating (labor) costs.

### *Inventory*

Inventory waste is the maintaining of more material than is required. The Gadget Shop made the business decision to order 15% extra stock to overcome the incidence of stock outages due to the weekly update of the central price and stock file. When The Gadget Shop was much smaller, this might have been a good business decision, but now that they have grown to the largest gadget shop in the industry, it is seriously hurting their business. Inventory waste is costing their business considerable expense in terms of stock write downs, and impacting the companies cash flow as a result of buying more stock than they really need to service their customer base. Additionally this practice increases their operating (labor) costs as a result of the effort for the warehouse to manage extra stock.

### *Motion*

Motion is the inefficient movement of workers within a business process. In The Gadget Shop, an example of motion waste is the warehouse staff taking the delivery advice documentation and giving it to the procurement department so they can attach it to the purchase order. The business impact of motion waste can be measured as increased cycle time and increases in operating (labor) costs.

### *Defects*

Defects waste is the Lean wastes associated with repair, rework, or scrap. This waste means that instead of performing the work right the first time it gets done twice (or thrice). As a Lean sales professional, be on the lookout for the prefix "re-." For example, retest, reinspect, recount, and of course rework. In The Gadget Shop, a defect waste example is the correction activities associated with the mistakes made during the manual data entry of the central stock and price file. These mistakes have resulted in stock being sold below The Gadget Shops cost price and impacted monthly and yearly profit margins.

### *Unused/Underutilized Talent*

Unused or underutilized talent is arguably the most destructive of all of the Lean wastes in that human potential and intellectual capital has gone untapped. It can result in staff feeling undervalued, which leads to poor staff morale and high employee attrition. An example of The Gadget Shop's unused talent waste is the activity of procurement personnel spending 8 hours to perform an administrative task. Instead of performing this nonvalue adding activity, their expertise could be better utilized negotiating better purchasing and contract terms with the Gadget Shop suppliers, which is their core skill set.

## *Identifying the Deadly Forms of Lean Wastes*

In the Lean selling methodology we develop a Value Stream Map (VSM) with the client team as a way of visually documenting the client's process. A VSM is fundamental in helping the client see the Lean wastes and how they are impacting their business processes and practices.

One of the main benefits of the VSM for a sales professional is that it helps the sales team to not only "see" the opportunities that exist within the client's organization, but it also helps the client to "see" them as well. The opportunities that the VSM exposes are described in terms of Lean wastes. These destructive wastes are specific forms of inefficiencies that detract from the end customer's user experience and also adds substantial costs to the end-to-end value stream. These forms of Lean wastes within The Gadget Shop will be further described once we have developed our VSM. Seeing deadly Lean wastes is the critical first step in solving the client's unique problem.

Often times, these wastes are hidden to the client's management primarily because the company does not fully understand the financial consequences of these waste. This situation in Lean terms is known as the "hidden factory," which is the unseen infrastructure and subprocesses that are put in place to deal with these costly wastes. Over time, process inefficiencies and "work-arounds" become common place, hence they are often overlooked and considered business as usual. One should not be misled by the term factory in the "hidden factory." While Lean has its origins in manufacturing, any industry and any process can possess a hidden factory. Typically, the magnitudes of these wastes are unknown and unquantified. The "hidden factory" gets its name from the fact that these costs are not captured by most accounting systems. Surprisingly, the financial impact to a customer can be and is typically quite significant. Uncovering these Lean wastes is the key to unlocking the "extrinsic value" that your client truly needs. Discovering the "hidden factory" is where you will need your client's support to gain access to the people who can help you develop the VSM. Fortunately, our SIPOC can point us to some of these key stakeholders and the process areas to include in our VSM interviews.

These interviews can be conducted individually, but it is far more effective if you can convince your client to arrange a time to meet with these key stakeholders and process owners, so that you can develop the VSM with them collectively in one VSM session. There is often an interesting dynamic that occurs during a VSM session. When representatives come together from operations across the end-to-end process, there is often an important shared discovery process that takes place on the part of the participants. More often than not, a member of an upstream process is unaware of activities taking place in a downstream process (and vice-versa). This discovery process is an eye-opener, and important for garnering buy-in for change across the entire value stream. The discovery process is even more profound when customer and supplier representatives are involved in the VSM session. The "ah-ha" moments are often times many and memorable. They uncover improvement opportunities for the client's business and present potential sales opportunities for the Lean sales professional.

The VSM can take on many altitudes from a 10,000 ft view from above the client's business to a very detailed view of the activities that take place within the process. Of course, the VSM is always more detailed than the SIPOC, as the SIPOC establishes a good "drill down" point for creating the VSM. A good rule of thumb for setting the appropriate altitude for your VSM is if you or your client feel there is an improvement opportunity in a particular process area, then go for a more detailed view of the activities taking place there, since effective process analysis almost always takes place at "ground level" within the process. For example, in our Gadget inventory management process, a large amount of manual data entry errors to the central price and stock file is noted as a cause of the long order to delivery cycle times; therefore, a detailed process analysis of the inventory management process is required to identify the root cause of the excessive central stock and price file errors. Lean selling requires that the sales professional takes a "go-see" approach to process analysis to observe the actual work being performed. Often times a client will describe the process as they believe it to be; however, the actual process is often much different and contains many forms of Lean waste.

It is important to point out that there are commonly two VSMs that a sales team will create: a "current state VSM" and a "future state VSM." The current state, or As-Is, VSM depicts the current process and identifies the Lean wastes that are inhibiting the flow of the end-to-end value chain. By eliminating or minimizing these wastes, a new and improved process will emerge, which is referred to as the future state, or To-Be, VSM. We will describe the future state

VSM in more detail in a future chapter as it is an important Lean selling method for making a compelling business case for your product or service to the client.

Another important point concerning the development of a VSM is the software that is used to develop one. While there are custom software tools and templates containing unique VSM icons and symbols, a number of PC office tools can be used to develop a VSM. Any presentation software, for example, can effectively illustrate a current and future state VSM. The key to an effective VSM is to illustrate the Lean wastes that exist in the current process and demonstrate the dramatic performance improvement in the future process by eliminating these deadly forms of waste. Figure 5.4 illustrates the current state VSM for The Gadget Shop's inventory management process, and Figure 5.5 also shows this 'as-is' VSM with the inclusion of "kaizen bursts." A kaizen (pronounced "ki' zen") burst denotes an improvement opportunity that exists in the current state process. These kaizen opportunities are improvement areas in the process where the Lean sales professional can target products or services to eradicate all the various forms of Lean wastes that exist.

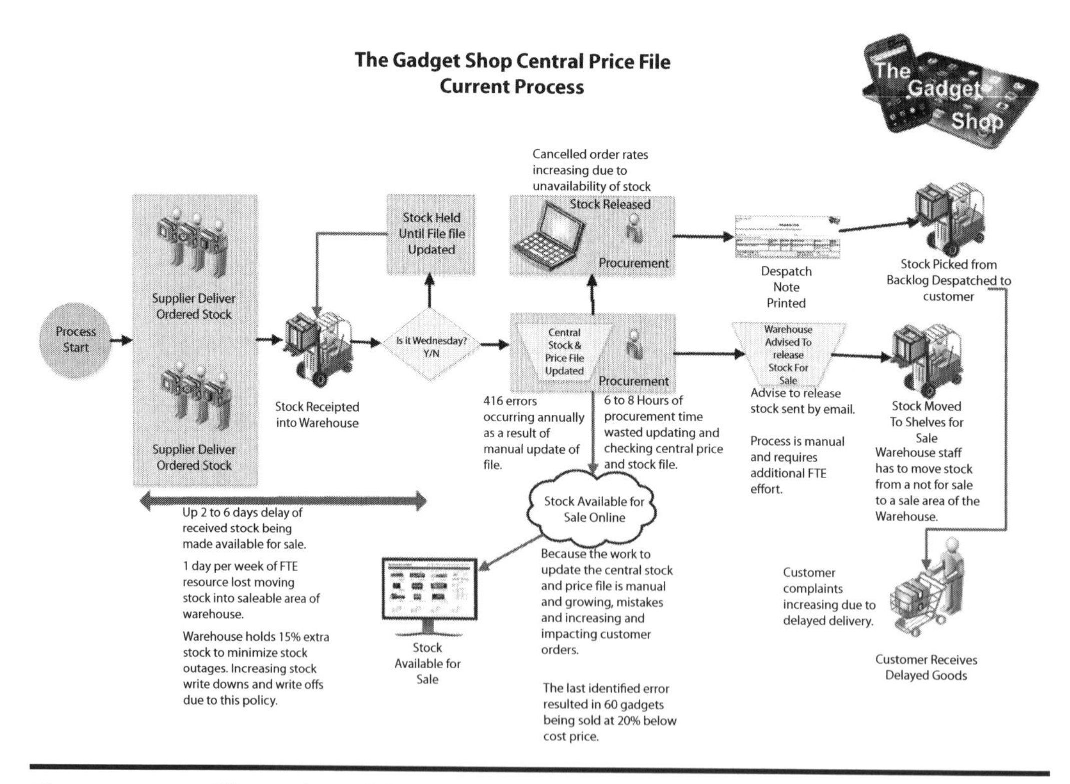


**Figure 5.4 An illustration of the current state VSM for The Gadget Shop's inventory management process.**

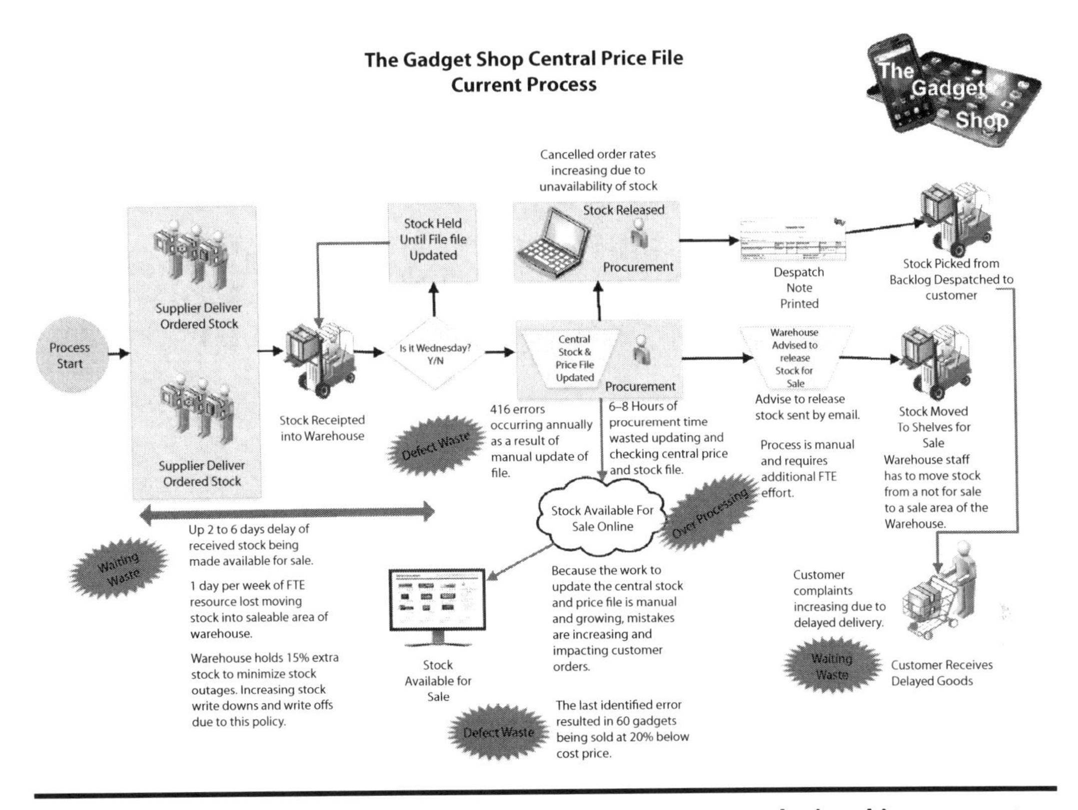


**Figure 5.5 The Gadget Shop inventory management process depicted in a current state value stream map with kaizen bursts identifying improvement areas.**

Once a VSM is created, the forms of Lean wastes should be identified. As previously discussed, there are eight forms of destructive Lean wastes that can exist in any process. In Figure 5.3, these eight forms of Lean wastes are illustrated and described in some detail. In most processes, these wastes (or, nonvalue added steps) comprise the vast majority of time spent within the process, whereas the value added steps comprise a vast minority of time spent within a process. When performing a process analysis on the VSM, a "value-add" analysis is performed for each process step. To be considered a "value-adding" process step, or activity, it must meet three criteria:

1. The customer is willing to pay for the inclusion of this activity in the process (and of course willing to pay for the resulting product or service).
2. The activity changes the form, fit, or function of the product or service.
3. The activity is done right the first time.

All three of these criteria must be met for a process step, or activity, to be considered value-adding. An example of a value-adding activity in The

Gadget Shop's inventory management process is "creating accurate updates to the price file" that ultimately passes the procurement team's "double check" verification for ensuring their inventory accuracy. A nonvalue adding activity in this process is the "double checking" of the manual entries since they should be entered correctly the first time and should not require any type of verification. Of course, the time spent by procurement fixing these errors in the stock file is also a "nonvalue added" activity. A nonvalue adding activity can also be described by using one of the eight forms of Lean waste. For example, correcting a database error such as a wrong price or inaccurate inventory quantity is classified as a form of "defect" waste that is associated with this nonvalue adding activity.

Highlighting these errors on the current state VSM is the role of the "kaizen burst." This burst is a graphical representation that resembles an "explosion" icon on the VSM; which is appropriate as everyone wants to "blow up" these Lean wastes as an metaphor for eliminating them. In Figure 5.5, the kaizen bursts highlight areas in the process where Lean wastes are having a detrimental effect on the current process. These bursts help the client to "see" the wastes, and they are the key focus areas for process improvement that target the deadly forms of Lean wastes that are present in the client's process. The elimination of these wastes gives rise to the future state VSM, where the impact of these wastes have been either completely removed or greatly minimized. This waste elimination, either directly or indirectly, addresses the root cause of the client's problem and helps them realize their business goals.

Once the kaizen opportunities and wastes are made visible to the client, the Lean sales professional should embark upon determining the impact that these wastes are having on the client's business. This impact assessment in Lean selling terms is referred to as a "capability study." It is called a capability study because it outlines the capabilities that a client requires in order to achieve its business objectives. A completed capability study creates the platform for the sales professional to provide a solution for delivering extrinsic value to their client. In Table 5.1, the Lean wastes in The Gadget Shop's inventory management process are described, along with the business and financial impact resulting from these wastes.

During the capability study, the Lean sales professional identifies the forms of wastes found in the client's business process, and for each waste the business and financial impacts are identified, quantified, and documented. These impacts are, of course, determined in collaboration with the client team. The Lean sales professional becomes skilled at situational questions pertaining to a particular waste in a client's process. For example,

**Table 5.1 The Gadget Shop's Lean Process Capability Study**

| *Lean Waste* | *Description* | *Business Impact* | *Financial Impact* |
|---|---|---|---|
| **Defect Waste** | Manual data entry errors that have resulted in stock being sold below cost | Stock sold to customers before data entry was identified. Error resulted in The Gadget Shop selling 600 units of product before the mistake was identified | Data entry mistakes cost $20,000 over last year |
| **Overprocessing Waste** | Manual vs. automated data entry | The manual data entry for stock and price updates take around 8 hours once each week | Approx. $20,000 per year of labor costs |
| **Waiting Waste** | Stock waits to be placed into a "ready for sale" warehouse location | The Gadget Shop inventory systems do not reflect the physical inventory that resides within the company, resulting in the need to carrying 15% excess inventory | See inventory waste financial impact |
| **Transportation Waste** | Receipted stock is moved from a "not for sale" to "ready for sale" area in the warehouse | Each week thousands of items are moved from one or to the other in the warehouse, resulting in 654,000 ft of excessive material transport per year | The time for warehouse resource to move these items each week equates to around $115,000 per quarter |
| **Inventory Waste** | Carrying 15% of extra stock | The inventory carrying costs are creating a cash flow problem for The Gadget Shop | The cost impact is $115,000 per quarter |
| **Motion Waste** | Sending warehouse receipts to procurement for data entry | As supplier shipments are received daily, the receiving dock personnel are hand carrying stock receipt lists to procurement taking around 4 hr/day | The labor cost to hand carry the stock receipt lists to procurement is approx. $15,000 per year |

(*Continued*)

**Table 5.1 (Continued) The Gadget Shop's Lean Process Capability Study**

| *Lean Waste* | *Description* | *Business Impact* | *Financial Impact* |
|---|---|---|---|
| **Unused Talent Waste** | The procurement team is entering and verifying the stock and price database | Instead of spending 8 hr/wk to negotiate better pricing and more favorable terms and conditions from its suppliers, The Gadget Shop procurement team is entering and checking data | The financial impact is unknown; however, The Gadget Shop management team has several supplier programs that require procurement's time and attention |
| **Overproduction** | Popular Gadget Shop items are picked from stock and packaged awaiting a firm customer order | There is warehouse and shipping labor expended on packing in advance of an order. Many orders are unpacked and returned to stock as new version of items are received | The labor cost to The Gadget Shop is approx. $10,000 per year |

in The Gadget Shop there is defect waste that results from manual data entry errors in the central stock and price file. The Lean sales professional will ask questions such as "how often do these errors occur?," "how and when are these errors detected?," "who first detects the error?", "what is the impact to the business when an error happens?," and "what actions is the business taking to prevent these errors from recurring?" Most sales professionals are already quite skilled in these questioning techniques, and in Lean they are referred to as the "What, Why, Where, When, Who and How" questioning method that helps to scope a client's problem to confirm its 'point of cause'. The point of cause is not the problem's root cause, but rather a bounded area within the process for performing a thorough root cause analysis.

In the Gadget Shop scenario, a recent pricing input error caused the company to sell 600 items below cost, resulting in $20,000 of lost revenue for their business. This is an example of a hard financial impact that the sales person can use to make a business case when offering the client a proposed solution. Additionally, The Gadget Shop has put in place a "double check" of the data inputs by the procurement team. Remember that a recheck (or re-"anything," for that matter) is a form of defect waste and in this particular case, it is employee talent waste as well. Instead of negotiating better prices or more favorable supply agreements for The Gadget Shop, a procurement employee is checking the work of another employee. The cost of this verification activity can also be calculated. The sales professional can identify how frequently the rechecks are performed, how long they take, and how many employees are needed to complete them. Now, since The Gadget Shop pays the procurement employee regardless of the type of work performed, this cost is therefore considered a "soft" business impact. The business of these "soft" savings is still of great value to the client, as their ultimate goal for The Gadget Shop is to sell gadgets more quickly, less expensively, and at a profit.

The capability study will complete this type of business impact analysis for each form of Lean waste that is identified in the VSM, and should be documented in a fashion similar to Table 5.1 and then validated with the client. The client now recognizes the impact that these Lean wastes are having on their processes, and sees the business imperative for resolving their problem. Furthermore, the quantification of the overall system impact of this and all the other deadly Lean wastes will be described further in Chapter 7; where Lean selling expands upon how to build an effective business case that compels the client (and their entire organization) to make the proposed changes.

In preparation for building a business case that compels the client to act (and hopefully purchase the solution that you are recommending) it is helpful at this point to begin organizing the Lean wastes identified into the balanced scorecard categories. Recall that the original goal statement for this client engagement consisted of balance scorecard success measures. To review, the balanced scorecard categories include quantitative and measurable improvements to the: client's experience, financial performance, business process performance and people (employee) learning and growth. By mapping the specific Lean wastes (those that the Lean sales professional has helped the client team identify) to the balanced scorecard components, this activity begins building a business case that is unique and personal to your client and to their business. Hence, the Lean sales professional has now begun successfully identifying and quantifying how their products and services deliver "extrinsic" value to the customer. The client can now clearly see how Lean selling provides products and services that deliver quantified value to their business.

It is important to note that not every problem or their root causes are going to lead to a sale, but more often than not they do. And even when they do not, you have created an important and lasting bond with your client, as you have demonstrated to them that their best interests are your interests as well. The next time your client is faced with a serious business problem, they will start calling upon you to see if your line of products and services can help them solve it. This is a welcomed "role reversal" for any sales team, and a true testimony to your becoming a trusted advisor to your client. Thanks to these Lean techniques being introduced into the sales engagement, a sales professional can now become that trusted advisor in a unique and profound way.

# Chapter 6

# Getting to the Root Cause of a Client's Problem and Proposing the "To-Be" Process

> Any fool can make things bigger, more complex, and more violent. It takes a touch of genius—and a lot of courage—to move in the opposite direction.
>
> **Albert Einstein**

Now that the deadly forms of Lean wastes are identified and the destructive wastes quantified in the clients process. The sales team work is not quite finished. In fact, there is a key and critical next step that the sales team must facilitate with the help of the client. The next step for the sales team is to show and demonstrate that your products and services will alleviate the damaging impacts of the confirmed and agreed upon wastes. In other words, the next part of the sales engagement is to work to identify the root cause, or causes, of these wastes and offer a solution that addresses those causes. Figure 6.1 shows the progress made on the Lean sales funnel and as you will see, we are progressing through its final stages but our work is not quite finished.

Much has been written about root cause analysis along with the many tools and techniques for determining a root cause. Here, we will discuss the more effective tools that can be applied in the sales engagement to identify the root causes creating the customer's problem; in this case, we are identifying the source of the client's Lean wastes. The two techniques of choice for root cause analysis are the Ishikawa (or fishbone) diagram

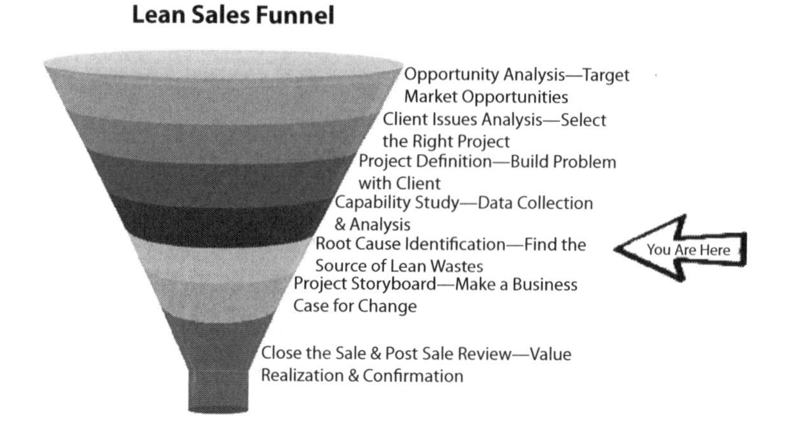


**Figure 6.1 Lean sales funnel highlighting root cause analysis stage.**

and the 5-Why analysis. Of course, garnering support from the client and select members of the client's team is paramount for performing the root cause analysis. At this stage the customer is typically "bought in" and will do everything in their power to provide every bit of assistance to help the sales team get to the heart of their problem.

It doesn't matter how long you have worked in the business world; nearly everybody has experienced a business process or practice that creates a recurring problem. Often in Lean selling, the customer engagement will identify aspects of a problem where the company has implemented a "quick fix" in hope of resolving the problem, only to find the problem resurfacing weeks or months down the road. An example of this scenario within The Gadget Shop is the fact that the company holds 15% extra stock to buffer against their untimely inventory updates. Over the past few years, as The Gadget Shop has grown in popularity, the amount of time it is taking them to manually update their central stock and price file has increased as well. In an attempt to minimize the impact to Gadget's customers, a decision was made to order 15% extra inventory. This decision was a way of containing the problem that the manual updating of the price file was having on stock availability and The Gadget Shop's sales revenue. It did not, however, fix the root cause of their problem and at best, it masked it by covering up for the untimely stock updates by actually creating Lean inventory waste. The issue with a short-term fix for any business is not knowing exactly how that fix ultimately affects the one key stakeholder that keeps them in business — the customer. At first glance, while holding 15% extra stock appears to overcome the problem, it is possible that the customer is still impacted by out of stock items, and this impact is creating ongoing damage to The Gadget Shop's reputation and future growth.

In Lean, there is a common saying: "You can't inspect quality into a process," which is derived from a quote originally attributed to total quality management guru, W. Edwards Deming (1900–1993). At the heart of Lean is the principle of "quality at the source." This represents the idea that additional inspections to ensure quality are not value added to the business. If a business process has wastes at a certain stage, the cost of waste is always incurred, whether it is inspected or not. "Quality at the source" ensures that quality output is measured at both the end of the process and also at every step of the business process. This ensures that there is minimal defects at the end and we built in quality incrementally from the beginning of the process to the end. It is common in non-Lean domains to see organizations build inspection points into a process, and in many cases they even have multiple inspection points. This tendency to add inspections at will is primarily because in today's fast-paced business world there is constant pressure to fix problems quickly and move on to the next challenge. There is always pressure on managers and employees to keep the business moving forward at all costs. In Lean selling, however, our mantra is to "go slow, to go fast." A Lean sales professional takes the time needed to understand the process in sufficient detail and to identify the root causes that are the underlying reason for the process being inefficient and ineffective. Lean selling helps focus your customer's business on making quality at the source an integral part of everything they do.

During the Lean selling engagement, our collaborative goal is all about getting past the symptoms of your customer's problems in order to find a permanent fix. Fortunately, performing a root cause analysis with your client is not all that time consuming. In a relatively short meeting with the client's team, which involves the same group who participated in the supplier-inputs-process-outputs-customer (SIPOC) diagramming effort (discussed in Chapter 5), a sales professional can conduct an effective root cause analysis session that includes the fishbone diagram as well as a thorough 5-Why analysis.

One of the most effective tools for performing a root cause analysis is the fishbone diagram, which is illustrated in Figure 6.2. The fishbone diagram was first introduced by Dr. Kaoru Ishikawa in 1968. His tools were quickly embraced by the business world, as a critically important technique used to help teams identify potential causes of the serious problems that their business was facing. As you can see from the illustration in Figure 6.2, a fishbone diagram does not have to be overly complicated; yet, it is very effective at getting beyond symptoms to identify the actionable root cause

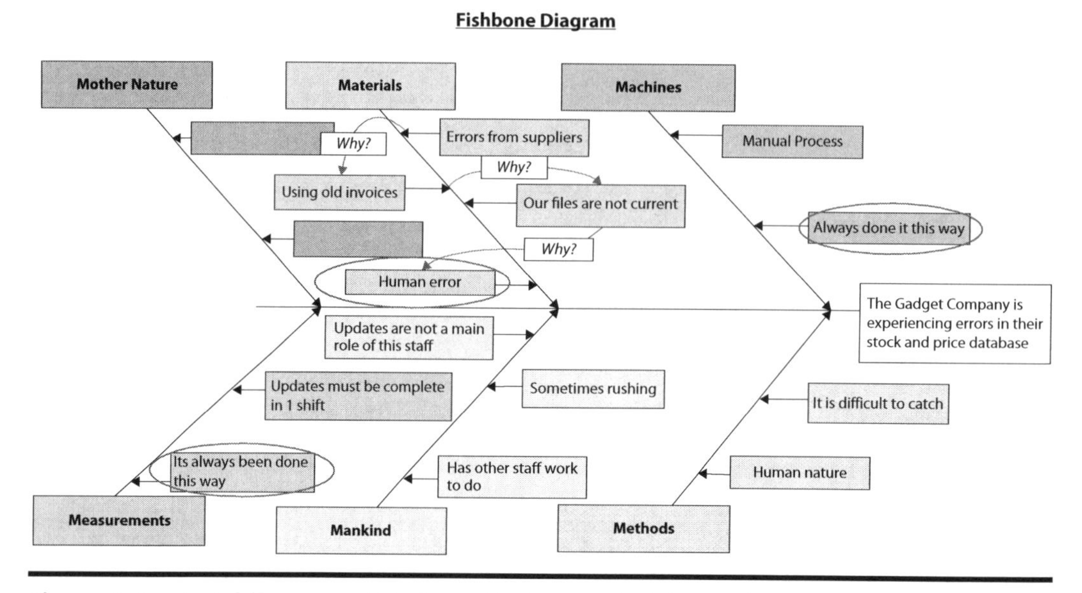


**Figure 6.2 An Ishikawa, or "fishbone," diagram for The Gadget Shop's stock and price database errors.**

or causes for a particular problem. The term "actionable" root causes means those causes identified by the team as the ones which the team believes they can control or influence. In documenting the root causes the team agree which causes to "act" upon. There can be just one actionable root cause that surfaces during a fishbone activity; however, it is far more common for the team to identify several causes to act upon, as most problems are complex and are rarely the result of just one cause.

When constructing an Ishikawa diagram, the problem statement is always located in the "head" of the fish, and good convention dictates (and honors the standard set by Dr. Ishikawa) to always illustrate the head of the fishbone diagram on the right-hand side of the diagram. It is useful to remember that the Ishikawa fish always swims from left to right. The "bones" located on the left-hand side of the fishbone diagram are used to identify potential causes of the problem that is documented in the head of the fish.

Another important aspect of the fishbone diagram is its "causal categories." Causal categories are often used as the headings for the "major bones" of the fishbone diagram. Causal categories are general areas in a business where the root cause(s) of a problem might be found. The cause categories listed in Figure 6.2 are the 6Ms that are commonly used in a manufacturing and industrial setting. These cause categories are also further described in Table 6.1. It should also be noted that causal categories can be customized so that they reflect the type of business area that you are working in. Table 6.2 describes the 6P causal categories that can also be used in a services industry Ishikawa diagram. Effective cause categories should cover the broad spectrum of business areas where the causes of a problem may originate. They are intended to help the team direct their thoughts during their brainstorming activities to the sources of potential root causes. Not only do they help the sales team organize the sources of potential root causes by categorizing them, the cause categories can help prompt a potential root cause by focusing the team's attention toward a specific area of the business. For example, during root cause analysis the team can ask themselves, "How do Supply issues effect our problem?"

Typically, the sales and client teams begin the root cause analysis process by brainstorming any and every potential root cause of a problem, and they simply locate those causes within the cause categories that best fits that potential root cause. For example, the Lean sales professional will ask the client team "Why do you think your company is experiencing low website traffic?" One client team member may respond with "poor server availability" as a potential cause, which gets documented within the fishbone diagram under the cause category of "Machine" or, in other words, the technology used to support the process. Other potential causes are brainstormed by the client team and the sales professional captures those causes within the appropriate cause category on the Ishikawa diagram. An "empty" cause category, meaning one without any potential causes, is not uncommon; however, it should serve as an alert to the sales team to prompt the client team for further brainstorming of the causes related to this particular area. Often times, an additional potential root cause or two will surface which allows for a more comprehensive analysis, and ultimately better solutions.

It should be noted that there are several common causal categories that are widely used during the root cause analysis process, and usually depends on the nature of the problem being addressed as well as the type of business or industry segment that you are working in. A popular set of cause categories is commonly referred to as the 6Ms, since each causal area begins with the letter "M," which helps the team quickly recall these cause categories when constructing their Ishikawa diagram. In the manufacturing sector, some commonly used cause categories are listed in Table 6.1.

Similar to the 6Ms for the manufacturing sector, the nonmanufacturing industry segments embrace some commonly used cause categories that are similar to but slightly different than those used in a production environment. For example, an IT application development process might use a services Ishikawa diagram with its unique causal categories that illustrate the

**Table 6.1 An Ishikawa Diagram's Cause Categories for a Manufacturing Company**

| *Cause Category* | *Description* |
|---|---|
| **Mankind** | People causes of the problem. Commonly, skills and training causes are listed in this category. |
| **Machine** | Machine, systems, and/or technology sources for the problem. A common cause here may be poor equipment reliability causing a defect or system delay. |
| **Materials** | Supply used in the process that may be the source of the problem. Any item provided to the core process is considered in this category. |
| **Methods** | Processes and procedures that may be the cause of the problem. Typically, antiquated or ineffective procedures are listed here as causes. |
| **Measurement** | Key business performance measurements that promote undesirable behaviors, or inaccurate measurements are causes listed in this category. |
| **Mother Nature** | Environmental factors or any "outside" factors that may be a cause of the problem are listed in this category. |

potential sources of the destructive forms of Lean wastes that existed within that particular current state process. The service Ishikawa diagram uses a 6P convention for its cause categories. In Table 6.2, the 6P cause categories are described for the services industries along with a specific example for The Gadget Shop new order fulfillment process.

Often times, the first few causes identified by the client team during the Ishikawa brainstorming session do not address the root cause(s) of the problem. In fact, many of the potential causes are merely symptoms and do not reflect a cause that will prevent the problem from resurfacing in the future. Using Lean tools and techniques to move beyond symptoms, and to document the root causes that are impacting a customer's business is what makes Lean and Lean selling so effective. In a sales engagement, a collaborative root cause analysis discussion is what makes Lean selling unique, and it is a key differentiator that will lead to closing more deals and delivering more value to the client. An effective Lean tool that we use to delve beyond symptom's is the "5-Why?" technique. This technique is extremely useful in terms of getting beyond an initial problem and its symptoms in order to uncover a root cause or root causes.

**Table 6.2 An Ishikawa Diagram's Cause Categories for a Services Company**

| *Cause Category* | *Description* |
|---|---|
| **People** | People causes of the problem. Commonly, skills and training causes are listed in this category. For Example The Gadget Shop staff spent up to 8 hours updating and checking the central stock and price file. Because they do this they are not utilising their skills to find new and innovative suppliers and improved pricing. |
| **Policy** | Policies or business rules as potential sources of the problem. The Gadget Shop policy of holding 15% extra stock is ensuring that when customers order gadgets that they are available in stock. |
| **Practices** | Practices or informal procedures that may be the source of the problem. The practice of moving receipted goods into the "Not for Sale" holding area delays selling products to customers and takes up valuable warehouse space. |
| **Procedures** | Processes and procedures that may be the cause of the problem. The Gadget Shop procurement department cannot begin to update the central stock and price file until the warehouse staff manually deliver the receipted goods paperwork. Time is then taken to manually staple the receipted goods form to the purchase order. |
| **Performance Metrics** | Key business performance measurements that promote undesirable behaviors, or inaccurate measurements are causes listed in this category. For example because the Gadget Shop has no measurement of the number supplier orders placed week to week, and the central stock and price fill process is manual, it is next to impossible to accurately measure stock rotation cycle times. |
| **Plant** | Plant issues or any "broader" factors that may be a cause of the problem are listed in this category. The Gadget Shop Commerce Software has no facility to automatically update stock and current purchase price. |

The root cause analysis conversation with the client is where the 5-Why technique can be quite useful for delving beyond a problem and its symptoms in order to uncover a root cause. As its name implies, the 5-Why method asks the question "Why" five times in order to surface the root cause. In practice, the question "Why" may be asked less than five times and possibly even more than five times. As a rule, the client and sales teams stops asking "Why" when they identify a cause that is ultimately outside of the team's control or influence. An example of the 5-Why method for The Gadget Shop's inventory management process is depicted in the following illustration:

**Problem:** There are multiple errors in The Gadget Shop's central stock and price file.

**Question:** Why are there multiple errors in the central stock and price file? (Why #1)
**Answer:** *Because they are created during the manual data entry process.*
**Question:** Why are they being created during manual data entry? (Why #2)
**Answer:** *Because the printout procurement is getting from the goods receipting department is sometimes illegible.*
**Question:** Why are the printouts sometimes illegible? (Why #3)
**Answer:** *Because the printer was low on ink at the time they were printed.*
**Question:** Why are the printers low on ink? (Why #4)
**Answer:** *Because the goods receipting department uses the printer for printing out many other Gadget Shop documents.*
**Question:** Why does the goods receipting department use this printer for printing other documents? (Why #5)
**Answer:** *Because it is the only printer the goods receipting departments has in their area.*
**Question:** Why is there only one printer in the receiving area? (Why #6)
**Answer:** Because it has always been that way. ***STOP!*** *This is either not actionable and/or beyond the team's control, so back up to the previous cause.*

**Actionable Root Cause:** *There is only one printer in the good receipting area and it is used for printing multiple documents; therefore, the procurement printouts are sometimes illegible.*

**Potential Solution (i.e., Lean Countermeasure):** Procurement will add a dedicated printer to the goods receipting department for the printing of their stock and price documents, and the goods receipting personnel is will verify the documents for legibility prior to delivering them to procurement.

Now, let us assume in our Gadget inventory management example that another one of the actionable root causes is determined to be the inherent inaccuracies of a manual data entry process causing the errors in the central stock and price file. The Lean sales professional then leads the client team in the process of brainstorming solutions that address these root causes. For example, an automated, web-based inventory management system might be one proposed solution to this specific root cause. The term "countermeasure" is used to describe any recommended solution that addresses a root cause. A countermeasure is a solution or action taken that "counters" the ill effects of a root cause, and of course the term "measure" is synonymous with "means"; which is the approach taken to address the problem.

Other recommended countermeasures are identified during brainstorming and captured by the sales team. It is important to point out that not all root causes or recommended solutions are ones that the sales professional can remedy with a product or service that they sell. Typically, based on past sales experience, there will always be some aspect of a product or service that can be applied to the root cause. This is one of the reasons why Lean selling is so powerful because it enables the sales team to have early insight that qualifies the likelihood of delivering the proposed solution to the customer. In other words, very early in the sales cycle, a sales team will know whether or not they have an offering that might be able to help the client. Of course, they are not certain they can help them until the sales team confirms the root cause with the client team.

Even if the worst case scenario occurs and the root cause does not align to your product or service, then the time spent to get to this point in the Lean selling cycle is typically far less than the time expended during a traditional sales cycle. Additionally, the relationship built with the customer up to this point in the sale process will ensure that even if you cannot assist them today, then you will be asked back to help them tomorrow. In fact, clients often have a level of skepticism about a sales professional and the sales teams using Lean for sales in their engagements because typically sales professionals have a vested interest in selling something. Lean puts the customer first, as we always listen to the "voice of the customer," and when Lean selling principles are applied, then the client will move past skepticism and real open collaboration can begin. Furthermore, close rates for deals are always higher when using Lean selling compared with those sales people using more traditional methods. The honest assertion is that Lean sales professionals are truly looking for the best solution for their client regardless of whether or not it leads to a sale.

A Lean sales professional always demonstrates the "principle of giving" versus the all too common "perception of taking," which is the stigma that has been known to plague many traditional sellers. Of course, the sales professional's motivation is to close a sale with this client; it is, after all, their job to sell products. However, Lean principles put the needs of the clients first, so the primary job of Lean sales professionals is to solve their clients' problems. Ultimately, the Lean selling approach leads to building a much strongerclient relationship and one that is founded on mutual trust.

In terms of selecting the appropriate countermeasure or countermeasures for the client, the Lean sales professional continues to document all the recommended solutions until all the actionable root causes have been addressed with at least one countermeasure. At this point, there may be several countermeasures that the client is considering, and with so many choices it can be overwhelming for the client team to narrow down this long list of countermeasures to the critical few that will alleviate the vast majority of their pain. (i.e., the 80/20 rule in Lean selling)

Fortunately, the Lean sales professional has another weapon in their arsenal of collaboration techniques, and the weapon of choice for this particular situation is called a "solution selection matrix," or simply a "2 × 2 matrix." Using a 2 × 2 matrix, the sales professional applies criteria-based decision making with the client team to narrow down this broad list of potential countermeasures to the appropriate few to be implemented. The term "2 × 2" originates from the fact that the matrix uses two distinct decision criteria for each recommended countermeasure, which are as follows:

1. Value
2. Time to value

These criteria are used to evaluate all countermeasures at two (2) levels, high and low, for each of the two criteria. If more granularity between the high or low ratings is required to distinguish between all the recommended countermeasures, then an ordinal (ordered numbers) rating scale can be used. For example, using a 1–5 point scale, called the Likert scale, can be a useful approach. Applying the Likert scale where a rating of 1 equates to a very low rating, 2 is low, 3 is moderate, 4 is high, and 5 equates to a very high rating for each of the two criteria (value and time to value). Other ordinal scales can be used as well, such as a 1–10 rating system, depending on the degree of granularity required and differentiation needed to distinguish between all the countermeasures contained within the 2 × 2 matrix. Most commonly used is the Likert scale and it is typically quite effective in terms of differentiating among all proposed countermeasures.

In Figure 6.3, a solution selection 2 × 2 matrix is illustrated for The Gadget Shop's inventory management example. The 2 × 2 matrix is used by the Lean sales professional to help the client team select the most appropriate countermeasure(s) by using both the "value" and "time to value" ratings

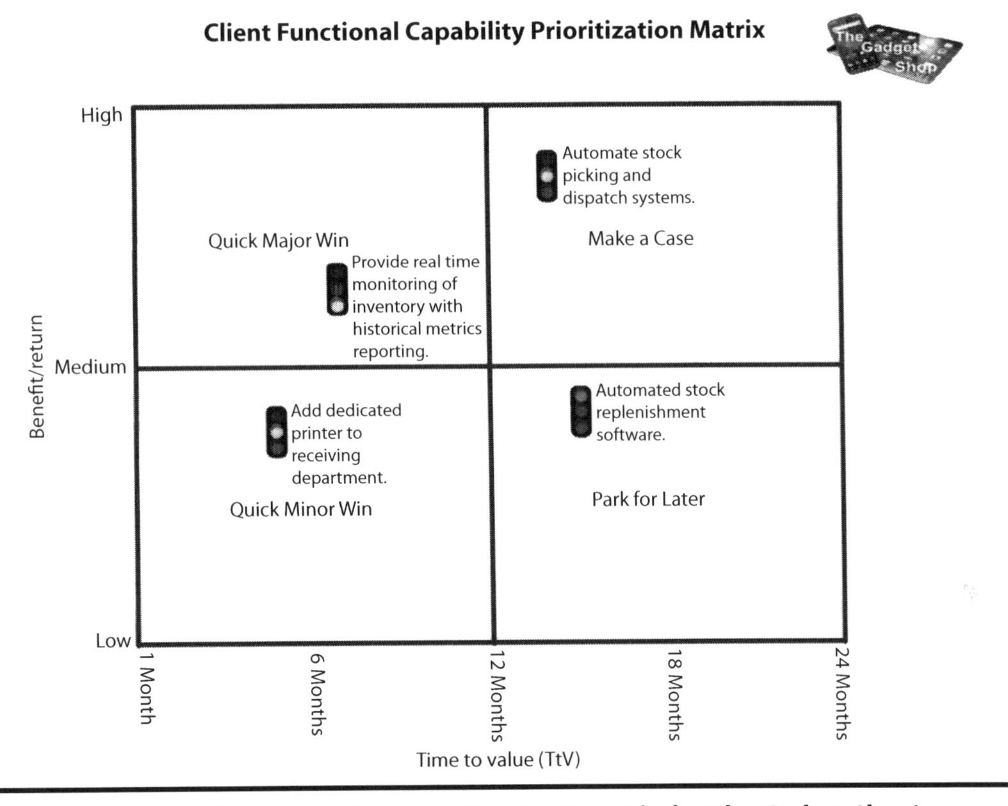


**Figure 6.3 Example of a solution selection 2 x 2 matrix for The Gadget Shop's inventory management process.**

for each countermeasure, and then the team can evaluate its position in the 2 × 2 matrix. The matrix lends itself to be readily segmented into four quadrants and a countermeasure's location within a quadrant helps to support the sales and client team's decisions. For example, the "park for later" quadrant indicates a countermeasure that has a relatively low value with a relatively high time to value; meaning that it will take a long time to deliver a fairly low benefit; so these countermeasures are 'parked' for a future consideration. The "quick minor wins" quadrant may include a countermeasure that the team might select, since its time to value is fairly quick; however, no countermeasure is considered in isolation. In other words, a "quick minor win" countermeasure will not be selected if it diverts time, attention, and resource away from a countermeasure that yields a higher client value, especially if it delivers that higher value in the same or less time.

It may be obvious at this point that the ideal quadrant in the 2 × 2 matrix is the "quick major win" quadrant. This quadrant contains countermeasures with a relatively high "value" rating and relatively low "time to value" rating;

so a very good business benefit can be realized in a fairly short period of time. It is also important to note that the countermeasures in the "make a case" quadrant should not be ignored. This quadrant contains countermeasures that deliver a high value, but take longer to realize this value compared with those in the "quick major wins" quadrant. In fact, the "make a case" quadrant might even contain a countermeasure that delivers the highest value to the client. A business case, however, will need to be made by way of a business justification, or cost/benefit analysis, for recommended solutions in this quadrant. In fact, the sales professional can use all the information that has been gathered and confirmed by the client thus far in order to make that case. In this book, we will further describe how to leverage Lean selling techniques to make that compelling business case for the client.

It is also important to note that in addition to *value* and *time to value* as criteria for the solution selection matrix, there is at least one more decision criteria that can be used. Adding more criteria and information is often useful in terms of supporting the team's decision process. In Figure 6.3, the 2 × 2 has "colored traffic light" icons, or symbols, associated with each one of the countermeasures relative to this third criterion; which in this case is "strategic alignment" to the client's business objectives. Shapes, sizes, or colors can be used to include additional decision criteria, if the sales and client teams so desire. However, there is a strong caution about using too many decision criteria, as it could over-complicate the selection of appropriate solutions, wherein the team gets trapped within the "analysis paralysis" syndrome. Typically, two or three criteria are sufficient for supporting the team's solution selection decision making process.

Using colored icons is a commonly used technique for including other decision criteria. This 2 × 2 matrix uses the colors red, yellow, and green traffic light icons to depict the criteria of "strategic alignment" for each countermeasure. Specifically, the "red light" denotes a "weak" alignment to the client business strategies, a "yellow light" indicates a "moderate" strategic alignment, and a "green light" illustrates a "strong" alignment to the client's business strategies. Now, the team can evaluate all the countermeasures using this criterion as well as the other two criteria. For example, a countermeasure with a "low" rating in "time to value" (meaning it will take a relatively short time) may have a "moderate" strategic alignment, whereas a different countermeasure with a higher "time to value" rating (meaning value is realized later than the aforementioned countermeasure) may have a "strong" strategic alignment rating. The team may decide that the countermeasure with the "strong" strategic alignment rating is the one to select, since it does a better job at helping the company achieve its strategic objectives.

The client team now must use the 2 × 2 matrix to decide which countermeasures to move forward. The matrix is known as a decision support tool in that the matrix does not make the decision for the sales and client teams, but rather it supports the decision making process. The team will need to reach consensus on the countermeasures they feel are the most appropriate for the client's business, and of course select the ones that will ultimately resolve the problem by correcting the root causes. Once the client team reaches consensus on their countermeasures of choice, the Lean sales professional has yet another Lean technique to apply before completing this important stage of the Lean sales cycle.

This next step is to define the client's future state process, so that the client team and other key stakeholders can visualize what their "To-Be" process will look like once these countermeasures are implemented. Visualizing the To-Be, or future, state is a critical step toward gaining the client's buy-in. A tangible illustration of the new process is a powerful technique for rallying the client team and key stakeholders around the proposed process changes. A skilled Lean sales professional will illustrate how the introduction of their products and services helps the client to realize this new and improved process. Figure 6.4 illustrates a future state process scenario for The Gadget Shop's inventory management process. Notice that the deadly forms of Lean wastes have been removed or dramatically minimized in the Gadget's future state process. The future state value stream map helps the sales and client teams visualize what their client's business will look like once the Lean sales professional's solutions are implemented.

Of course, the specific business benefits of the To-Be process still need to be quantified by the sales and client teams, but most of the hard work has already been done. One approach to building a business case for change is for the project team to assign a dollar value to the Lean wastes that were eliminated or minimized as a result of the proposed solution(s). Much of this work has already been done by virtue of the client capability study described in Chapter 5. One interesting fact about the Lean selling approach is that because the level of collaboration between the sales and the customer teams, and because the engagement has enabled the identification of root causes, the solution offered by the sales team will always aligned to customer priorities. Why is this alignment always the case? Because, the Lean sales professional starts with a problem and goal that are in support of a client's strategy, so it stands to reason that the solutions to these problems will align to their

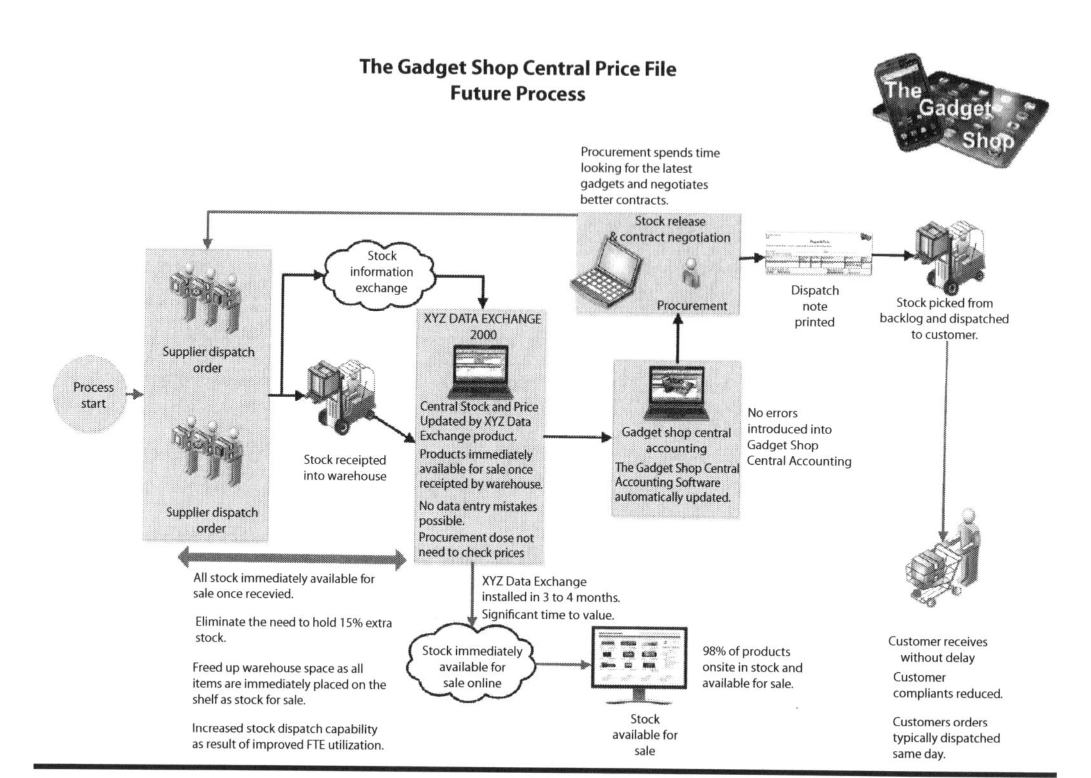


**Figure 6.4 The Gadget Shop's future state process map with the Lean wastes minimized or eliminated.**

business imperatives as well. Working in this way ultimately reduces a sales organization's operating costs, sales team size, and sales engagement duration. Indirectly, the Lean selling approach streamlines and "leans out" the sales operations while improving the client's business processes as well.

More will be discussed in subsequent chapters about building the client's business case for making meaningful change. By illustrating time to value for your proposed solutions and by creating the final value proposition by way of a Lean selling storyboard, the sales professional makes a compelling case to motivate the client to change from their current situation to a future state where significantly less waste exists in the business process. Chapter 9 outlines the development of a Lean storyboard, but first the Lean sales professional needs to identify all the insidious and destructive impacts that Lean wastes can have on a business. Chapter 7 helps the Lean sales professional to uncover the detrimental effects that the eight Lean wastes are having on your client's business. These effects are determined and documented by quantifying their financial impact on the client.

# Chapter 7

# The Cascade Effect and the Lean Selling Balanced Scorecard

A man should look for what is, and not for what he thinks should be.

**Albert Einstein**

Lean wastes in a process can have a number of consequences that can often go unchecked and not measured. This unfortunate oversight is simply because at first glance the impact of the waste can seem very small and insignificant. The reality is that, more often than not, even the smallest waste in a business process can have significant financial and business consequences. The full impact of this waste is often not well known nor well documented. In Lean terminology, this cumulative effect of Lean wastes is called the "hidden factory"; which impacts customers, incurs additional operating costs to a business operation, increases employee effort, and adversely affects operational efficiencies.

## Understanding the Consequences of Lean Wastes—"The Cascade Effect"

In Lean selling, this unforeseen chain of events that a Lean waste can have on a business and its customers along with its cumulative consequences is referred to as the "cascade effect." The term the "cascade effect" is used because it accurately describes an ever increasing business impact caused by the Lean waste downstream in the business process. Hence, a Lean waste that at first glance starts off small, can have a compounding effect as the unit of work progresses along the end-to-end process; thus creating a very real and significant financial cost for its business.

Documenting the consequences of Lean wastes is one of the key strengths of Lean selling. As a result of all the excellent Lean selling work that has been completed thus far with a customer, the Lean approach clearly helps to document the client's current state process. The various forms of Lean wastes in the current state are classified, quantified, and confirmed by the client. The classification of wastes enables a sales professional to comprehend the waste in terms of its impact on cost, quality, and operating efficiency. By identifying the relevant form of the eight Lean wastes, it becomes easier to assign the effect that a waste can have on a process, and in particular, it can help to quantify the financial consequences of that particular waste. Hence, Lean selling enables clear insight beyond the symptoms resulting from a customer's problems, and it enables the identification of a problem's root cause(s). The deliverable that can be presented to a client is a document that details the detrimental effects that their Lean wastes, both large and small, are having on their business. Even a seemingly minor form of waste can set off a chain of events that accumulate into a very significant and damaging financial impact on a client's business.

## Creating a Shared Understanding of the Consequences of Wastes—An Illustration

To provide an example of the cascade effect, lets us continue with The Gadget Shop example. Having previously met with the owner and staff of this up and coming on-line retailer in the technology market place. We know that they sell the latest and greatest must-have gadgets via an on-line retail channel. The Gadget Shop has a sales strategy that is focused on selling its products using a high volume and low profit margin business model. They have grown significantly over time; as a result of the great products, they sell at everyday low prices. As part of the Lean selling engagement, the customer's current state process has been mapped and the Lean wastes categorized. During the current state process analysis, it was noted that an important operation within the company's inventory management process requires significant manual effort.

The manual effort identified during the current state process analysis relates to the time it takes to manually update Gadget's central price list and stock file. Interestingly enough, there is a long history of this process being manual in nature. The manual effort required to perform the updating of the central price list goes back to when the owner first started The Gadget Shop. When the company was started several years ago, the number of product lines held by The Gadget Shop was small and the turnover was relatively low; so the manual process worked well. In the last 12 months, however, the number of product lines offered has dramatically increased and so has the product turnover.

The central price list file is a vital part of the The Gadget Shop's business, as it lists the current sale price of products brought into stock and the opening stock levels. This file ensures that online customers visiting the store are purchasing at a competitive price and that the stock availability is accurate. If the prices in the master price and stock file are incorrect, then depending on the type of error, it could affect the owner's profit margin. For example, if prices are loaded too high, that could result in Gadget advertising products on their website where their price is not competitive compared with their competition. If the item price is entered too low, then Gadget profits will be compromised, and items could be sold below cost causing a serious financial situation. Finally, if stock levels in the file are incorrect that can result in Gadget taking an order that cannot be fulfilled because insufficient or zero stock levels actually exist. Conversely, when stock levels are erroneously deflated then Gadget will incur the costs of carrying stock on their shelves, but no orders are coming in because stock appears to be unavailable.

The owners of The Gadget Shop believe that the cost impact resulting from the manually update to the central price and stock file is very low and is a fairly efficient way to run their business. As part of the current state process analysis, the manual update of the file has been categorized as "over-processing" waste (one of the eight Lean wastes) and can take one member of the team up to 6 hours per week to complete. The owner of the company has a member of the procurement team assigned to complete this manual update each and every week. From their narrow vantage point, The Gadget Shop is probably accurate in their analysis, as the operating costs associated with paying an existing member of staff to update the central price and stock file are relatively low. Furthermore, the owner does not believe that changing their approach to managing the central stock and price file is worth pursuing. After all, The Gadget Shop has always manually updated the central price and stock file because it is the most economical way to update the online pricing for companies of The Gadget Shop's size with a comparable product turnover rate.

This illustration is a perfect example of why the use of Lean can be so vital to the world of sales. Lean enables a sales organization to document the chain of events, that is, the cascade effect and demonstrate the impact of manually updating the company's price and stock file. Lean enables the accurate measurement of that cascade effect and the impact that it is having on the business so that the real cost to the company's online sales can be determined. A historical review of the last 6 months of the weekly update process for the central price and stock file has found that defects are quite common. This high-error rate is a result of the large amount of manual data entry to be performed in order to complete the task in 6 hours, which is the time allotted for the procurement employees to complete the work. On average, there are eight data entry mistakes (defect waste) made every week, which equates to 416 errors generated annually. In the last year alone, there have been two occasions where data entry mistakes resulted in products being sold to online customers below The Gadget Shop's purchase cost.

Apart from the risk of a data entry error costing the company money, there are additional operating costs associated with the procurement department having to fix these errors once there are identified. The time to correct these errors (also defect waste) needs to be captured and quantified as well. Additionally, to minimize these errors, the procurement department spends an additional 2 hours checking the updates for the week based on a recently instituted "buddy check" system to combat these manual entry errors.

In order to minimize the cost of updating the file and to prevent any disruption to sales, the central price and stock file is only updated midweek on a Wednesday. New stock is typically received into the warehouse every business day, Monday through Friday (expect for holidays). Assuming stock is received on a Monday for a product that is currently out of stock, then that item would not get loaded into the central file and made available for sale to customer until Wednesday; so the inventory levels are inaccurate for 2 days. If stock is received on Thursday for an item that is out of stock, which occurs after the weekly update, then it could result in stock not being made available for sale for up to 6 days. Of course, this delay in making available stock visible to The Gadget Shop's customers results in a loss in revenue. The consequence of customer orders being delayed for between 2 and 6 days is a significant part of the "Hidden Factory". This delay is further relevant as this business is an online store that sells its gadgets to customers 24 hours a day, 7 days a week. After discussing the effects that this particular problem is having on The Gadget Shop sales, it is obvious that the The Gadget Shop business team are not measuring how many sales are being lost as a result of this 2–6 days delay. To counter the adverse effects of their updating the central file only once a week; the company has traditionally ordered 15% more stock than required by sales demand; so they ensure of "buffer" inventory is on hand at all times.

This model for managing stock has historically worked fairly well; except that in the last 6–12 months the stock levels are not able to keep up with customer demand. To counter these increases in stock outages, the company has started to order new stock earlier than normal and when current stock numbers are still at reasonable levels. This advanced ordering (which is the Lean waste of overproduction) has helped to reduce the total numbers of items out of stock, but has placed an additional burden on cash flow because they are now ordering a larger quantity of stock far earlier than normal.

Finally, in the last 6 months, the company has seen a dramatic increase in the number of customer complaints and order cancellations that they believe are related to pricing issues, and customers experiencing prolonged periods of time waiting for their orders to be delivered. Based on the work that the Lean sales team has performed to document the client's current state process, it has been identified that the weekly update of the central pricing and stock file creates a cascade effect, which has a larger financial and end customer impact than The Gadget Shop originally thought. Based on the Lean sales teams analysis, the following conclusions are documented and agreed with the client team.

## The Impacts of the Cascade Effect

1. Procurement spends upwards of 6 hours per week updating the central pricing and stock file. An additional 2 hours is spent cross checking the manual entries for accuracy. Despite this cross check, data entry errors still make it onto the online sales site.
2. Because the update to the central stock and price file is manual, and with an increasing number of complex changes made each week; this is resulting in several errors consistently found each and every week. On

average, there are eight mistakes identified during the "buddy check" and these require time for correction each week. Despite spending time to find the errors, a few still make it through to the on-line website. Last year, a particular data entry error resulted in stock being sold below cost. This one error alone cost the company in a significant amount of unrealized revenue and lost profits.

3. Depending on when new stock arrives at Gadget's warehouse, it can take between 2 and 6 days to be manually loaded to the website and made available for sale. The estimated lost sales from this delay in loading stock are difficult to confirm, but based on customer buying patterns, it is possible to estimate the annual loss of revenue and gross profits.
4. The policy of purchasing and carrying 15% extra stock levels as way of ensuring that the company does not run out of stock impacts the company's cash flow and operating expenses. Additionally, this last year the company had to write off or send to clearance stock a number of product lines that were superseded by newer products. The cost to the company associated with this impact to cash flow as well as the write off of stock can also be calculated.
5. Finally, the company has seen an increase in cancelled orders per month of around 1% due to stock unavailability and delivery timeframes. The number of the cancelled orders has risen to 50 orders per month, which is resulting in a loss of revenue and gross profits. The number of customer complaints has also increased from two per month, to five per month. Based on the fact the customer's business is online and the documented complaints have risen to five per month, then the suspicion is that the total number of unhappy Gadget customers has probably doubled.

Since the Lean selling professional has taken the time to document the customer's current state process, and has begun to measure the consequences of the cascade effect, and has validated the root causes of the deadly Lean wastes, it is now possible to document the effects that these wastes are having on The Gadget Shop's day to day business operations. In par-ticular, it is now possible to quantify the financial impact of the wastes by quantifying the lost revenue and increased operating expenses. Measuring the impact that the Lean wastes are having on The Gadget Shop's top and bottom lines makes it possible to quantify their impact on customer service.

## Quantifying the Value—Building a Balanced Business Case

Now, having clearly documented the customer's current state process, along with a proposed future state process, the sales team can assist the customer to achieve their specified goals. The question now becomes how to deliver on that goal and enable the customer's vision for the future. The reality is that removing the waste from the customer's current process and delivering the future state will take time, resources, and money. Where should the Lean sales team start? The first question the sales professional must answer is "How can the products and services that he or she offers serve as an enabler to the client's future state process, and help them realize a confirmed payback or return on their investment?" The answer lies in breaking down the client's current state process to a level of detail so that the cost and consequences of their Lean wastes can be confirmed. Understanding the actual cost of these wastes and the consequences they are having on the The Gadget Shop's business and on their customers allows for more intelligent decisions to be made. Specifically, decisions concerning the first steps toward The Gadget Shop's future state process are of primary importance at this stage of the sales cycle.

This analysis is vital as there may be some really simple things that can be done to contain the waste while a longer term and permanent solution is being implemented. These immediate actions are referred to as "containment actions" as they contain a problem's impact until a preventive and permanent action can be implemented. As an example, the online gadget retailer could update the central price and stock file twice a week as an interim measure until a more automated solution is implemented. Of course, this measure is not the ideal and final solution since this containment action will add more operating costs to the The Gadget Shop's business. Additionally, the aim of Lean selling is to identify the 20% of a product or service that will address 80% of the Lean wastes and deliver the majority of the value in the shortest possible time (within 1–12 months). Identifying those 20% of the client's Lean wastes is another outcome of root cause analysis; which not only allows for permanent solutions, but also helps the sales professional identify those solutions that will have the greatest impact on the client's problem. After all, minimizing the business impact of a client's problem with the least possible investment and in the shortest possible time is what Lean selling is all about. Finally, when the sales team presents a plan about what should be done first and the value it will enable in the customer's future state process will give the client much more confidence in the sales proposal. It should become evident that the sales team is not looking to sell as much as they possibly can as quickly as possible, but rather they are looking to solve the client's problem as efficiently and effectively as possible. Subsequently, the Lean sales professional is continuing to earn the client's trust.

In building a balanced business case, the sales teams role is to work with the client's data, that is, ensuring that it is as accurate as possible and aligns with the unique needs of that client's business. The balanced business case should be "personal" to that specific customer, based on actual client data, and not based on the sales team's subjectivity that could lead to proposing an entirely wrong solution for this important client. While building the balanced business case, the sales team uses the "so what" test. In other words, "so what" is the impact to the client's business as a result of having this waste in their process?

This test uncovers the real business implications of the Lean wastes that the sales professional has captured during the current state process evaluation. If, upon the review of the business implications and financial impact of the identified wastes, you can ask yourself "So what is the impact to the client's business?" (And, the answer is not completely obvious from your impact statement), then rework the financial or business impact statement until such time it is relevant and real to your customer. The "so what" test is an enabler to continuous qualification of a balanced business case, and often times requires the sales team to circle back with the client to clarify possible business implications caused by the Lean wastes. It also ensures that the approach taken is not overly optimistic or biased, in that the impact statements are iteratively refined and reviewed with the client until they are accurate, and ultimately confirmed by the customer.

To break down the client's Lean wastes and their consequences and to begin assigning costs, initially the Lean wastes in a client's process must be identified and classified into waste categories. In working with the business owner and staff of the The Gadget Shop to understand their current state process, it is possible to quantify the financial consequences of manually updating the central price and stock file. The impact that this operation is having on the on-line retailer's business and to its customers can and must be quantified. To begin building a balanced business case, the identified wastes are organized into categories. A waste category is a classification heading that categorizes that particular waste. Depending on your client's industry, and the products or services they sell, these category perspectives may differ slightly. These categories reflect Kaplan's and Norton's (1995) Balanced Scorecard for measuring business success (using customer, financial, process, and people success measures) with an additional category for employee innovation: which draws upon the Lean principle of empowering employees and minimizing employee talent waste.

The following are examples of typical balanced waste categories.

## *Financial Category*

The financial category includes business impact measures such as increased operating costs, or loss of revenue. For example, the real costs associated with the manufacture of a defective product. These are the costs associated with paying staff to do additional rework to fix the defective product or resolve any recurring problem. Another example could be the revenue lost as a result of not getting to market in time to take advantage of a market opportunity. Table 7.1 illustrates this financial component of the balanced business impact of the Lean wastes.

## *External Customer*

External customer performance measures are any impact to the customer in the context of the external customers' satisfaction, their likelihood to recommend, market share growth or decline (also a financial impact) and cancelled orders. The reduction in repeat business (this is a financial category, but can also be an indicator of customer and market acceptance of products and services). Table 7.2 illustrates this external customer component of the balanced business impact of the Lean wastes.

## *Internal Customers (Employees and Stakeholders)*

Internal customer impact statements measure the satisfaction of the staff in dealing with the consequences created by the Lean waste. For example, the impact that dealing with unhappy customers can have on employee job satisfaction. Or employees having to perform manual and repetitive tasks that impact their likelihood to remain in their roles. Unhappy workers can have an unintended negative impact on the external customer engagements as well. Table 7.3 illustrates this internal customer component of the balanced business impact of the Lean wastes.

**Table 7.1 Financial Impact of the Balanced Scorecard**

| *ScoreCard* | *Problem's Identified* | *Identified Outcomes of Problems* | *Measurement Category* | *Measurement Units* | *Measurement System* | *Average Annual Costs* | *3 Year Cost* | *Projected 3 Year Cost* | *Proposed Save Percentage* | *Proposed Annual Savings* |
|---|---|---|---|---|---|---|---|---|---|---|
| Financial: | The Gadget Shop current policy to avoid stock outages is to purchase 15% extra stock. Although this policy was valuable when the company had a small turnover. Today it is creating an increased cash flow burden on the company | The policy of holding 15% extra stock is costing the company $100,000 a month in increased operating costs. Additionally due to increased cash flow on occasions the company incurs interest on an overdraft as a result of insufficient liquid funds to pay for new stock at time of ordering. | Hard Dollar | Increased Operating Costs | USD | $1,200,000 | 3 | $3,600,000 | 100.00% | $3,600,000 |
| Financial: | The increased stock levels have resulted in more stock having to be sold at clearance. This is due to stock being superseded by a newer models prior to turning over current stock. | Reduction in gross margin impacts company profitability as a result of increased frequency of stock write offs. | Hard Dollar | Increased stock write off and revenue loss | USD | $50,000.00 | 3 | $150,000.00 | 60.00% | $60,000.00 |

(Continued)

**Table 7.1 (Continued) Financial Impact of the Balanced Scorecard**

| *ScoreCard* | *Problem's Identified* | *Identified Outcomes of Problems* | *Measurement Category* | *Measurement Units* | *Measurement System* | *Average Annual Costs* | *3 Year Cost* | *Projected 3 Year Cost* | *Proposed Save Percentage* | *Proposed Annual Savings* |
|---|---|---|---|---|---|---|---|---|---|---|
| Financial: | A manual error in updating the central price and stock file resulted in stock being sold below cost during the last financial year. The pricing mistake was not identified until a significant quantity of stock had been sold. Products sold at the incorrect price had to be honored. | Errors in manually entering the price and stock details resulting in products being sold below cost the sold price. Sales had to be honored and resulted in 60 gadgets sold at 20% below purchase price. | Hard Dollar | Loss of Sales | USD | $20,000.00 | 1 | $20,000.00 | 100.00% | $20,000.00 |

**Table 7.2 External Customer Impact of the Balanced Scorecard**

| *ScoreCard* | *Problem's Identified* | *Identified Outcomes of Problems* | *Measurement Category* | *Measurement Units* | *Measurement System* | *Average Annual Costs* | *3 Year Cost* | *Projected 3 Year Cost* | *Proposed Save Percentage* | *Proposed Annual Savings* |
|---|---|---|---|---|---|---|---|---|---|---|
| External Customers: | The Gadget Shop's website indicates products to be out of stock when stock is available and in their warehouse. It is not just loading information into the central stock and price file. | Sales lost due to stock availability. Lost sales are estimated cost the company $10,000 per month. | Hard Dollar | Loss of Sales | Sales turnover rates | $10,000.00 | 3 | $30,000.00 | 40.00% | $12,000.00 |
| External Customers: | Customer with orders for gadgets on back order can wait an additional 2 to 6 days for stock to be dispatched. | Increased customer complaints and order cancellation. Estimated cost $2,000 per month | Hard Dollar | Complaints per month and loss of sales | Number of Complaints Month over Month Comparison | $2,000.00 | 3 | $6,000.00 | 40.00% | $2,400.00 |
| External Customers: | The Gadget Shop has seen a significant increase in the number of customer complaints | Customer dissatisfaction and loss of sales | Risk to Brand | Customer Complaints | 2 % of annual sales | | | | | |

**Table 7.3 Internal Customer Impact of the Balanced Scorecard**

| *ScoreCard* | *Problem's Identified* | *Identified Outcomes of Problems* | *Measurement Category* | *Measurement Units* | *Measurement System* | *Average Annual Costs* | *3 Year Cost* | *Projected 3 Year Cost* | *Proposed Save Percentage* | *Proposed Annual Savings* |
|---|---|---|---|---|---|---|---|---|---|---|
| Internal Customers: | It takes 1 person up to 6 hours per week to update the central price and stock file. (procurement) | Cost to pay existing staff to complete the update. It costs $31.25 per hour at a fully burdened labor cost. | Soft Dollar | Increased Operating costs | Hours per year undertaken on no value added work | $9,750.00 | 3 | $29,250.00 | 90.00% | $26,325.00 |
| Internal Customers: | Additional 2 hours per week to check entries and fix all mistakes (procurement) | Additional time and effort required to check file inhibits procurement from undertaking more value added takes. | Soft Dollar | Increased Operating costs | Hours per year undertaken on no value added work | $3,250.00 | 3 | $9,750.00 | 10.00% | $975.00 |

### *Business Processes*

Business process impact statements measure the cost, throughput, and/or cycle time of the process under investigation. In this category, the sales team documents how well an end to end business process performs for a production, procurement, order fulfillment, or any business process. Table 7.4 illustrates this business process component of the balanced business impact of the Lean wastes.

### *Intellectual Capital*

The intellectual capital impact is a measurement of arguably one of the worst and destructive consequence of the Lean wastes. This is a measure of the impact waste can have on innovation, new ideas, creativity, and continuous improvement. The sales team must document any waste that inhibits staff from the freedom to enable innovation, delight customers, simplify processes, and improve customer service. Table 7.5 illustrates this component of the balance business impact of the Lean wastes.

## The Gadget Shop: The Lean Wastes Identified and Their Business Impact Quantified

Once the wastes and their impact have been grouped into the appropriate categories, then the problems associated with the central price and stock file can be further broken down to detail the impact that these problems are having on the online retail business and its day to day operations. It is the ill effects of these Lean wastes that impacts customers, inhibits business growth, and ultimately costs The Gadget Shop significant revenue/profits. It is also these documented effects of the wastes and their financial impacts that the sales professional's product or service is going to reduce, if not eliminate. In particular, the balanced business case is going to indicate exactly how the proposed product or service will remove the customer's waste and deliver and net financial improvement. This level of detail is vital if the business case is going to be personal to the customer and to their unique business. Table 7.6 calls out the proposed hard and soft business impacts of the Lean wastes found within The Gadget Shop.

The ultimate goal of Lean selling is to build a business case that shows the customer the extrinsic value of the proposed product and service. Extrinsic value is the portion of an offering's net worth to a client's business

**Table 7.4 Business Process Impact of the Balanced Scorecard**

| *ScoreCard* | *Problem's Identified* | *Identified Outcomes of Problems* | *Measurement Category* | *Measurement Units* | *Measurement System* | *Average Annual Costs* | *3 Year Cost* | *Projected 3 Year Cost* | *Proposed Save Percentage* | *Proposed Annual Savings* |
|---|---|---|---|---|---|---|---|---|---|---|
| Process: | Sending warehouse receipts to Procurement for data entry | As supplier shipments are received daily, the receiving dock personnel are hand delivering the shipment notes to procurement for loading on central stock and price file | Soft Dollar | Increased Operating Costs | Hours per year undertaken on no value added work | $15,000.00 | 3 | $45,000.00 | 10.00% | $4,500.00 |

**Table 7.5 Intellectual Capital Impact of the Balanced Scorecard**

| *ScoreCard* | *Problem's Identified* | *Identified Outcomes of Problems* | *Measurement Category* | *Measurement Units* | *Measurement System* | *Average Annual Costs* | *3 Year Cost* | *Projected 3 Year Cost* | *Proposed Save Percentage* | *Proposed Annual Savings* |
|---|---|---|---|---|---|---|---|---|---|---|
| Intellectual Waste | Manual entry every week is mundane and not an efficient use of procurement resources. | Staff find manual update of central price and stock file boring and repetitive | Risk to Brand | Procurement productivity | | | | | | |
| Intellectual Waste | Procurements time not spent on real value added procurement activities like improving supplier portfolio and credit terms. | Staff should be spending time negotiation better stock purchases deals | Opportunity Loss | Improving buying power | USD Savings made on improved credit terms and supplier discounts. | | | | | $100,000.00 |

that is agreed and assigned to it by external factors. These factors are typically external to the product or service itself, and they are specific to the customer and their business. Based on The Gadget Shop and its online business, from a financial category perspective, three problems have been identified. The business outcomes created by the problems are then further quantified to identify the real financial impact that the manual update of the central price and stock file is having on The Gadget Shop's business. An example of the business outcomes are shown in Table 7.7.

**Table 7.6 Hard and Soft Benefits Consolidated View**

| | |
|---|---|
| Proposed Hard Savings | $3,694,400 |
| Proposed Soft Savings | $131,800 |

**Table 7.7 Identified Business Outcomes**

| *Problems Identified (Defect Waste)* | *Identified Business Outcomes* |
|---|---|
| The Gadget Shop has a current policy of purchasing 15% extra stock to minimize stock outages caused by the manual update of the central price and stock file. This policy minimized outages when the company was smaller and had a lower inventory turnover. Today, it is creating a burden to the cash flow and is increasing the carrying costs of the excess inventory. | The policy of holding 15% extra stock is costing the company $100,000 a month in increased operating costs. Additionally, due to increased cash flow on occasions the company incurs interest on an overdraft as a result of insufficient liquid funds to pay for new stock at time of ordering. Last year, overdraft charges were over $24,000. |
| The increased stock levels have resulted in more stock having to be sold as clearance items. This clearance is due to stock being superseded by newer models before the current stock could be sold. | Reduction in gross margins impacts company profitability as a result of increased frequency of stock write offs. Clearance items are sold an average discount of 20% per item. A total of 10,000 items were sold on clearance last year resulting in over $50,000 of lost revenue opportunity. |
| An error caused when manually updating the central price and stock file resulted in stock being sold below cost. The pricing mistake was not identified until a significant quantity of stock had been sold. Products sold at the incorrect price have to be honored to maintain customer loyalty and satisfaction. | This last fiscal year, the manual error resulted in 60 gadgets being sold at 20% below cost price. This error cost The Gadget Shop $20,000. |

Breaking down problems into the business outcomes, or consequences, created by the Lean waste is a vital part of quantifying the impact in the context of financial, operating had human resourcing cost. Lean tools, such as, a cause and effect matrix, Ishikawa (or fishbone) diagram, and a failure modes and effects analysis (FMEA) can be used to assist in breaking down the problem to identify their causes and to ultimately understand the impact on the client's business. In Chapter 5, we have described the Ishikawa diagram to identify a problem's root cause(s). In addition, a sales professional can use Failure Modes Analysis (FMEA) and a Cause and Effect Matrix in their customer engagements. These analysis tools are not covered in this book, however there is a lot of information on these tools and techniques available on-line and books are dedicated to these subjects; which can be found in many readily available references and resources. These techniques will add depth and diversity to the Lean sales professional's tool box of useful problem solving skills.

## Measuring the Business Impact of a Problem and Its Associated Lean Wastes

Now that outcomes of the problems have been identified, it is possible to start identifying the best method for a financial impact assessment. In Lean selling, the following measurement categories are used:

**Hard Dollar:** The real financial consequence of the Lean waste resulting in an impact to the company's financial statement. Hard dollar measurements can include, but are not limited to, loss of sales, stock write offs, increased operating expenses, financial penalties, or interest. An example of a hard dollar financial cost is the fact that the online Gadget Shop is writing off stock that is superseded by newer models. These write offs only occur because they are carrying an increase in stock levels. The financial losses associated with having to sell stock at lower profit margins or below cost can be calculated as a direct consequence of the current business practice of carrying 15% more stock than is required.

**Soft Dollar:** Typically, the increase in operating costs associated with inefficient process and business practices. An example of a soft dollar impact is that our online Gadget Shop pays a member of its staff for 6–8 hours to manually update the central pricing and stock file. Their salary is a fixed cost to the business, so while we can calculate the employee's hourly rate to determine this cost, the employee's salary does not change.

Therefore, a financial report does not show the cost of this manual entry practice. The soft cost is no less important to The Gadget Shop. If we remove the need to spend 6–8 hours doing this work, this time could be reallocated to improve the terms and conditions associated with purchasing new gadgets. Perhaps, this time could also be spent negotiating a higher discount on the current stock being sold.

**Risk to Brand:** This is another soft measure, but it is related more to the impact a Lean waste can have on Gadget's customers and how it can hurt their reputation or image in the marketplace. In the case of our online retail business, there has been an increase in customer complaints and cancelled orders. Increases in order cancellations can be measured and can have a negative impact of future sales.

**Opportunity Loss:** The measure of a lost commercial opportunity as a result of a Lean waste and its business outcome. In the case of the online Gadget Shop, their practice of only updating the central price and stock file every Wednesday creates a measurable opportunity loss. This is a loss because depending on when stock is received it can take up to 6 days for new stock to be loaded for sale on the online system. The opportunity loss is in relation to sales revenue lost or orders not received as a consequence of stock not being made available for sale immediately once it is received. Figure 7.1 shows an illustration of a balanced scorecard.

| Score Card | Identified Outcomes of Problems | Measurement Category | Measurement Units | Measurement System |
|---|---|---|---|---|
| Financial: | The policy of holding 15% extra stock is costing the company $100,000 a month in increased operating costs. Additionally due to an increased cash flow on occasions the company incurs interest on an overdraft as a result of insufficient liquid funds to pay for new stock at time of ordering. | Hard dollar | Increased operating costs | USD |
| Financial: | Reduction in gross margin impacts company profitability as a result of increased frequency of stock write offs. | Hard dollar | Increased stock write off and revenue loss | USD |
| Financial: | Errors in manually entering the price and stock details resulting in products being sold below cost the sold price. Sales had to be honored and resulted in 60 gadgets sold at 20% below purchase price. | Hard dollar | Loss of sales | USD |

**Figure 7.1 Balanced business case measurement system example (financial impact).**

### *Measurements Unit*

The measurement units of the balanced scorecard are used to measure the size, frequency and ultimately, the costs associated with the consequences and business outcomes of the Lean waste. Measurement units can be lost revenue, loss of sales, costs of defecting customers, cost of marked down stock, and staff replacement.

### *Measurements System*

The measurement system is the set of units of measurement that will be used to quantify the measurement units identified. In Lean selling, it is typical for the measurement system to be financially specified in local currency. It can also be measured and quantified in the context of the number of errors and human hours required to fix the errors. As an example, Figure 7.2 shows an illustration in U.S. dollars.

## The Real Cost of Lean Waste (Building a Compelling Business Case)

The final part of building a balanced business case involves quantifying the costs in relation to the identified Lean wastes and the costs related to the business outcomes resulting from it. From the financial category perspective, one of the consequences of The Gadget Shop's business process of manually updating the central price and stock file results in the company purchasing 15% extra stock to minimize outages caused by the untimely manual update.

| Measurement Units | Measurement System | Average Annual Costs | 3 Year Cost | Projected 3 Year Cost | Proposed Save Percentage | Proposed Annual Savings |
|---|---|---|---|---|---|---|
| Increased operating costs | USD | $1,200,000.00 | 3 | $3,600,000.00 | 100.00% | $373,200.00 |
| Increased stock write off and revenue loss | USD | $50,000.00 | 3 | $150,000.00 | 60.00% | $60,000.00 |
| Loss of sales | USD | $20,000.00 | 1 | $20,000.00 | 100.00% | $20,000.00 |

**Figure 7.2 Balanced business case—Quantifying the cost of waste found at The Gadget Shop.**

With the online aspect of The Gadget Shop growing, it is holding 15% extra stock; which results in the company spending an additional $100,000 every month. Additionally, because of cash flow constraints, this policy costs the company an additional $24,000 per year in overdraft charges. Another consequence of the company holding 15% extra stock is that increased stock levels have resulted in more stock having to a sold as clearance. The need for clearance is due to stock being superseded by newer models prior to turning over the current stock. Stock write-offs this year has impacted gross profits by $50,000.

The third and final financial impact of manually updating the price and stock file is that last year an error occurred in the updating of the file. It took 48 hours for the error to be identified and during that time, the company sold a number of items at 20% below cost price. Products sold at the incorrect price had to be honored to maintain customer loyalty and satisfaction. This error cost the company $20,000 in gross profit. Today, as a result of the error, the procurement function takes more time to check the file update for errors. This double-check has added an additional 2 hours to the time to update the file each week, and it increases The Gadget Shop's operating costs. It also inhibits them from doing more value added tasks, which could help the company reduce costs and improve customer satisfaction.

In the context of the sales professionals balanced business case, in the last 3 years, the manual updating of the price and stock file has resulted in at least $3,000,000 of hard dollar costs. These costs impact profitability and ultimately affect the smooth delivery of customer service. Assuming that The Gadget Shop continues with the manual updating of the price file over 3 years, the costs and customer impact will be substantially higher. Our balanced business case will document exactly how the cost of these wastes will be eliminated.

## A Balanced Business Case for a Proposed Solution

As a sales professional, our engagement with the The Gadget Shop quickly identified that our products and services could enable the customer to eliminate the manual updating of the central price and stock file. This improvement is made possible by implementing a fully automated solution that takes price and stock information from the supplier and automatically updates the online store with the latest pricing and stock information. The only manual part of the business process to remain would be the receipting of stock into the warehouse. Once this improvement is complete, the latest price and stock levels are automatically released to the online store. This solution will only take 3–6 months to implement and deliver the following benefits:

1. Reduces up to 8 hours per week of 1 full time equivalent (FTE) procurements staff time.
2. Better utilizing employee skills and talents by refocusing 6–8 hours per week of procurement time to improving purchasing T&C's, discount levels, finding innovative new gadgets, and other procurement activities that increase company customer service and profitability.
3. By eliminating the purchase of 15% extra stock, the online company will improve its cash flow by $100,000 per month and save $24,400 per year in overdraft charges. This change will free up operating capital to invest in other revenue growth opportunities and customer service improvements. Additionally, the proposed solution will move the company to just in time stock holdings and reduce stock outage lead times by up to 80%.
4. By eliminating the purchasing of 15% extra stock The Gadget Shop would enable a annual saving of approximately $30,000 to $50,000 per year by significantly reducing the number of products sent to clearance and sold at a mark down price.
5. Reduces stock outage and stock delivery lead times by 90% over current levels as well as reducing the number of customer complaints regarding stock wait times. Grow new customer close rates by 2% annually.
6. Reduce or eliminate manual errors in The Gadget Shop procurement process. Automate the central price and stock function and eliminate errors related to manual entries. Delivering this automation will ensure that the online retailer is never again impacted by a $20,000 gross profit write off.

## Conclusion and Time to Value Revisited

Lean selling enables a sales professional to break down the client's problems into the context of Lean wastes and the business consequences of those wastes. It enables the sales professional to quantify the insidious "cascade effect" in great detail, and to effectively describe the real consequences that these wastes can have on a business and its customers. This level of detail is a unique enabler to align the extrinsic value of the product and service being sold with unique problem that a business is facing. The Lean sales professional solution is intended to remove the consequences of wastes and deliver to the client a competitive advantage, financial saving, and improved customer satisfaction. Working to this level of detail is a competitive advantage for the sales team, as it differentiates them from other sellers who do not expend the time and effort to thoroughly understand a client's problem. Lean sales professionals consistently win more business more often than traditional sellers.

By working with a customer in this manner, the sales team is demonstrating the *Principle of Giving*, and creating a relationship built on continuous collaboration with the client; as they are supporting the sales project every step of the way. The client supports the sale because they can clearly see how it benefits them. The balanced business case also ensures that the proposal is personal and relevant to the client.

The Lean wastes identified via Lean selling relate to the customer's business, and they are real to the client because they helped to uncover them. It has been stated many times in this book that *Value must be "Personal" to the Customer*. Whether the business is an individual proprietorship or a billion dollar corporation, the product being sold must deliver value that is personal to the client and recognized by other key stakeholders. Developing a specific problem and goal statement, mapping a client's current and future state processes, and building a balanced business case that quantifies hard and soft cost impacts to the client's business are all a means to making the sales teams solution personal for the client.

Finally, because of the time taken to understand the real consequences of waste, it is possible to align the product and service that is being sold in the context of time to value. Remember that a product of service is only ever valuable when it is consumed by the client. Hence, offering a customer a solution that provides a return on investment in 3 years after purchase is not very valuable. Time to value is a key differentiator for the Lean sales professional and one of the key tenets of Lean selling. Building a balanced business case and delivering a time to value that is meaningful to the client will be discussed in more detail in the next chapter.

## Reference

R.S. Kaplan and D.P. Norton. (1995). "Putting the balanced scorecard to work", *Performance Measurement, Management, and Appraisal Sourcebook*, Vol 66. HRD Press Massachusetts.

*Chapter 8*

# How to Build a Time to Value Proposition

> Logic will get you from A to B. Imagination will take you everywhere.
>
> **Albert Einstein**

## Introduction—How Does All This Lean Work Help to Sell a Product?

All the hard work has now been done by working with the customer, and now is the time to bring it all together by way of providing a value proposition. We started this client engagement as a journey, by working collaboratively with the client by first defining a problem and goal statement. The agreed upon problem statement must have a financial cost associated with it, and while those costs are not confirmed at the onset of the engagement, the Lean methodology helps to quantify and confirm those costs. The goal must also be specific and measureable, and it must include an expected timeframe to deliver the business benefit, along with a projection of the net financial gain realized by the client upon the delivery of the goal.

## Understanding Clients and Their Processes

As a Lean sales professional, the current state has been mapped using a high-level process map and all the cascading effects of the client's wastes have been illustrated. The net result of mapping the current state is that the joint team will have identified and confirmed a number of Lean wastes in the client's current process. In addition, the wastes have been quantified in the context of direct and indirect financial impacts. The outcome of this consultative work is gaining a clear insight into the financial impact created by the root causes, as well as identifying the other symptoms resulting from the client's business problem. Documenting the financial impact of this problem is vitally important, but arguably it is just as important to understand and document the consequences of these Lean wastes and their ill effects on the client's business, staff, and ultimately customers.

We have done some critically important work so far, but how does having all of this information translate into closing more sales, faster? First, It accelerates the sales cycle because from day one of the client engagement, the Lean sales team utilizes Lean techniques to start building a business proposal based on customer specific data. When comparing with a traditional sales effort, typically the business case is build toward the end of a client engagement. The Lean business case is not based on a number of assumptions that have been subjectively deduced based on other clients, or seemingly similar sales experiences, but rather the business value is confirmed by the client using information gleaned from their process. Additionally, the proposal is not based on industry standard metrics; such as, the average cost of a data breach, for example. Typically clients tend dismiss industry metrics as not relevant to their particular business. Finally, a typical Lean sales proposal tends to avoid using Total Cost of Ownership (TCO) or Total Cost of Acquisition (TCOA), as these approaches are based on a number of subjective estimates. TCO and TCOA proposals do not have enough detail to make them relevant and personal to a client. Client value is personal, and it does not matter whether you are an individual who is buying a new car or a multibillion dollar corporation acquiring a product or service in an effort to solve a business problem that delivers a competitive advantage.

## Collaborative Selling

In Lean selling, our sales proposals are personalized by working collaboratively with the customer, and they are based on real customer data provided by the customer, which is specific, unique, and relatable to the customer. The information for the Lean sales proposal has been collaboratively compiled, and continuously qualified for validity with the client. This successful value proposition is possible because the sales team continuously qualify and iteratively verify the proposal as it is incrementally developed throughout the engagement. Any assumptions in relation to the client's data are tested with the client team to confirm that they are at least 80% correct and not 100% wrong. The approach is not to achieve a perfect solution and one that completely satisfies 100% of the project's stakeholders, but rather provides significant facts and data from the client's process; so all decision makers can buy into the proposed solution. In other words, there is broad based agreement among a number of key stakeholders associated with the problem that the data and any associated assumptions are largely correct and have a significant financial impact on their business.

The ultimate goal of the Lean sales proposal is to deliver a document that is personal and relevant to the customer, pertinent to their unique business, and addresses the specific problems that are challenging them. Additionally, the Lean methodology enables the sales professional to deliver a detailed plan explaining how the proposed products and services will enable a competitive goal that the customer needs to achieve. This point is vital because any business case that a sales professional develops will be scrutinized by a wide array of people within the customer's organization. This review can include procurement, senior managers—such as the CEO and CFO—as well as numerous other decision makers and influencers. All of the stakeholders involved in the decision-making process to purchase could have significantly different agendas. Of course, they all have the best interests of the company at heart; however, different roles and functions are measured on different business outcomes. Consequently, some decision makers will be focused on costs, others on process and technology enhancements, while others will focus on value and financial business outcomes. Anybody who has been selling professionally for any length of time will tell you that navigating these agendas, personal or otherwise, is an integral part of achieving success in sales.

In Lean selling, your ability to align personal agendas and to positively influence their success is key and critical to closing the sale. Leveraging the client's own process data and demonstrating how their end-to-end process is significantly improved is foundational to achieving the broad based buy-in required to closing the deal. By the uncovering the existence of a real client problem and confirming its causes using real facts, the sales team now has the information required to garner broad based support. While documenting a client's problem, its business impact, and communicating how the proposed solution addresses the root cause is necessary, yet it is still not sufficient. A client and key decision makers need one more vital piece of information before they can make an informed buying decision. Specifically, a Lean selling proposal must clearly document the time frame when value can be consumed by the client, or in other words, Time to Value (TtV).

## Documenting Time to Value

Time to value (TtV) in Lean selling terms is the period of time it takes to eliminate the identified root causes and associated wastes from the customer's current state process, and to begin or complete the delivery of the improved future state process within a specified timeframe. Typically, in Lean selling it is our goal to confirm a favorable return to the client in less than 12 months. Cumulative returns are delivered over time; after the "quicker to remove wastes" are addressed, followed by more complex waste removal over time (2 or 3 years). It is the all-important time to value that makes Lean selling compelling to the customer. As an example, let us assume for a particular client that the sales professional has successfully identified the root causes of a problem within their current state process. After working with the customer collaboratively, it has been identified that the customer's current problems are costing $100 per year. The $100 cost has been calculated based on a number of Lean wastes that have been confirmed with the client team. The good news is that the products and services being sold by the sales professional will fix most of the customer's problems and eliminate a significant chunk of that $100 cost. Furthermore, the solution that the sales professional is proposing will only cost the customer $50. This is a great deal! Right?

The value proposition to the customer is that the proposed sales solution will eradicate most (if not all) of the $100 incurred each year by the customer, and all this benefit can be theirs for a capital investment of only

$50. The benefit to the customer is that over 5 years the customer's business would save in the neighborhood of $450 in operating costs after the deduction of the $50 in capital expense. On paper, this scenario looks compelling, but not in today's marketplace. In today's frugal business environment, clients are looking for physical proof of the net savings (i.e. they want to have cash in bank). Therefore, this approach is missing a vital ingredient. That ingredient is TtV. At the end of the day, it does not matter how good the product or service is that is being sold. The company selling the product or service may be the global market leader in the industry, or alternatively may be an organization consisting of only one person in an emerging product; they both need to present the same information to the client, which is time to value. Ultimately, the client is looking for the same thing from any sales engagement—value! Of course, they need to realize that financial return and the promised business value as quickly as humanly possible.

For a product or service to be valuable, the proposed solution being delivered must document exactly when the value can be delivered and realized by the client. In other words, when exactly will the client be able to recognize the net financial return on their investment? After all, value is only valuable once it has been received or consumed by the client. Unless clients have a clear understanding of exactly when the value can be consumed and what benefits they can expect to experience by consuming it, they will never feel confident in their financial return against the proposed capital expense. It is no longer good enough to present a proposal to a client with the perception or promise of value. This perception casts the seeds of doubt in the minds of the various client stakeholders, and their doubt decreases the likelihood of closing the sale. Every proposal must deal with the question of time to value and must describe exactly when the value derived from your product and service will be realized by the client.

Assuming that the sales team used Lean selling in an engagement and the client has agreed to the $100 operating cost as a result of a number of Lean wastes identified in their process, and they also support spending $50 on your proposed product or service, then the net result of your proposal confirms that in the first year the customer's business now has a $150 problem. This cost is incurred because in order for the client to realize any value their business must first make the capital investment of $50 before even $1 of Lean waste can be saved. With no time frame or plan to eliminate the $100 of Lean waste it is impossible to evaluate whether or not the $50 capital spent is a good investment. This situation can present a serious problem to the sales team because the client has to go to its executive and obtain capital approval for the organization to spend the $50 on the proposed solution before any of the $100 waste is removed. Typically today where stakeholders have doubts about the value and how it applies personally to their business, the answer will be "NO!". Remember it's better to be safe than sorry. This situation creates a risk in the minds of the customer's stakeholders and their attitude toward the value proposition may be skeptical. Personal reputations and accountabilities are often on the line to ensure that capital is spent wisely and that the project delivers a tangible business outcome with a net favorable financial return in an acceptable period of time. For this reason, it is critically important that the client understand the TtV associated with the expected business outcomes that the solution will enable.

Understanding the TtV allows the client to evaluate and compare the net return (up to $100 of annual operating cost savings) to the business in comparison to the capital outlay ($50). Enabling this tangible comparison is part of the wisdom of Lean selling. In Lean selling, our objective is to help the client team feel comfortable about making a capital outlay that will subsequently enable their business to see two or three times that expense in a net business return.

## Applying Pareto Principle in Lean Selling

In Lean selling, 80% of the time invested in our sales project is focused on documenting and quantifying the business consequences that result from a client's problem, therefore it enables a sales professional and the client to calculate the financial impact of the wastes. Additionally, the wastes and their solutions can be broken down within the context of time (TtV). Further, the Lean sales professional is able to identify which of the wastes should be removed first by proposing a specific product or service over other offerings that might also be available for sale. In other words, we use Lean principles to enable the sales team to identify the 20% of the client's problems that are causing 80% of their pain. This approach results in the proposed solution (a product or service) delivering 80% of the value to the customer by eliminating the right Lean waste at the right time. This approach will enable a net cost savings in an agreed upon time frame and one that works for the client. Specifically, what are the sales team's products and services that will eliminate the client's waste in 1–3 months, 3–6 months, 6–12 months, and greater than 12 months? Of course, the sales team hopes to eliminate most of the waste as quickly as possible. For example,

80% of the client's business benefit can be realized in the first 6 months, and the remaining 20% will be realized in 6–12 months.

Figure 8.1 illustrates how the sales professional's solution (products and services) can help to address the wastes that are hidden in the client's business processes. The letters "A" and "B" denote the beginning and the end of the process, respectively. The "peaks and valleys" in the figure represent when the process is running well (the peaks) and when costs are being incurred due to Lean wastes within the process (the valleys). The numbers #1, #2, and #3 in Figure 8.1 depicts the seller's ideas (products and services) that address these insidious wastes, the timeframe's to remove the measure wastes.

Now, let us look at a fairly simple time to value scenario for this fictitious customer with a $100 problem. What if the proposed solution could eliminate 60% of the waste in the first 90 days after product delivery? That improvement would result in the client being able to reduce the current $100 annual operating expense to $40 per year. Enabling TtV does require a sales organization to commit to the customer for the long term to enable the projected business outcomes. The sales company is starting a journey with the client to deliver their future state process. The net result of this work is a completed financial proposal to present to the client, as illustrated in Tables 8.1 through 8.3.

This commitment to confirm the client's time to value is at times not for the faint of heart, as the commitment to reduce the current operating expenses and deliver value within a certain time frame is a critically important commitment to the client.

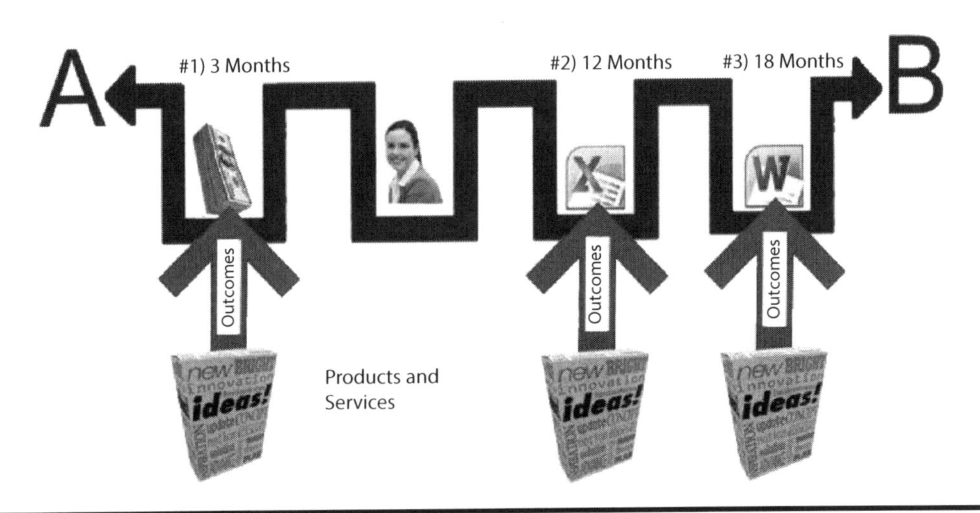


**Figure 8.1 An illustration of the "hidden factory" with problems, Lean wastes, and TtV for the proposed solutions.**

**Table 8.1 Net Operating Cost of Identified Wastes**

| *Wastes Identified* | *Cost* | *Timeframe to Eliminate Waste* |
|---|---|---|
| Order processing waste<br>*The current costs associated with the manual order data entry undertaken by XYZ Ltd.* | $60.00 | 60–90 days |
| Overtime to process orders<br>*The overtime expenses paid to staff annually to get all orders entered into the system.* | $20.00 | 90–120 days |
| Defects related to manual order entry<br>*The confirmed cost of operating expense needed to fix the errors identified in orders as a result of the manual data entry.* | $20.00 | 120 days+ |
| Total cost of waste | $100.00 | |

**Table 8.2 Net Operation Savings**

| *Delivered Solutions and Outcomes* | *Net Savings* | *Timeframe to Enable Automation and Remove the Waste* |
|---|---|---|
| *Automate the order processing to eliminate the current manual process* | $60.00 per annum | 70 days from implementation of solution |
| *Eliminate the need for overtime* | $20.00 per annum | 120 days from implementation of solution |
| *Eliminate errors in data entry.*<br>*Allowing for an 80% success rate in order entry errors removed as a result of automation* | $18.00 per annum | 120 days from implementation of solution |
| Total operating savings | $98.00 per annum | Delivered between 70 and 120 days from implementation |

The client will expect accountability from the sales team to deliver what has been agreed upon. Fortunately, a collaborative relationship has developed and matured over time, as both organizations have worked collaboratively throughout the Lean selling engagement. Both parties are keenly focused on identifying the client's Lean waste and realizing the business

**Table 8.3 Net Increase in Sales Revenue per Year**

| | | |
|---|---|---|
| Increased annual sales for 8 months as a result of order automation (after implementation) | $160.00 | Delivered between 70 and 120 days from implementation |
| Order processing automation provided by XYZ Ltd. delivered to ABC LLC | –$50.00 | Proposed implementation April 1, 2016 |
| Total increased sales revenue less capital investment delivered by August 2016 | $110.00 | |

value by removing these wastes. The Lean selling principle of "giving" will have ensured that the all important environment of trust has been created. Trust between both parties will ensure that collaboration will continue during the delivery phase of this project as well. The sales team must stay committed to their solution delivery until the client's future state process is realized.

## Expectation Management

Like every relationship, there will be ups and downs. As long as the interactions with the client continue to rely on Lean selling principles, then anything is possible. Interestingly, many companies do not take this approach to sales. There are many reasons why companies do not get to this level of detail and consequently their business cases end up being highly subjective. The primary reason is that most sales teams do not spend the time to document the problem and goal, the Lean wastes, their root causes, and the resulting business impacts. Not having this detail makes it nearly impossible to confirm Time to Value. There is a perception that getting to this level of detail will result in a prolonged sales cycle, and subsequently impact the seller's revenue stream. In fact, the exact opposite is true. When Lean selling is applied and time to value is delivered, the following things happen:

1. Close rates will increase dramatically.
2. Your clients' likelihood to recommend your company will increase.
3. Clients will ask for your company's involvement in a greater number of revenue generating projects.
4. Revenues from new sales will grow!

## Defining Value Using Lean Selling versus Traditional Sales—A Reflection

It is the goal of this book to describe the value that Lean principles can provide when utilized by a sales professional in the context of a sales engagement. The ideas described in this book are based on their successful use for some of the world's largest sales companies. In short, Lean selling and the application of Lean principles in sales really does work. After all, the profession of sales is all about successfully delivering products and services that enable client value. Delivering value is achieved by using client's process data to confirm that portion of a product's or service's net worth to a client. That worth is agreed upon by the client and is assigned to the product by external factors (i.e. the unique value it delivers to a specific customer, or its extrinsic value).

In the historical realm of sales, it would have been common that an exchange for a good or service was as a simple transaction. In other words, one party agrees to provide another party something in exchange for something else in return. Today, sales is more about providing value well beyond the price that a client is willing to pay for a good or service, and it does not really matter what you are selling. You could be selling cars, real estate, computers, software, or jet planes. If you work in sales, then typically, there will be one thing that you have in common with all other sales professionals: your primary role is to engage with the customer and conclude that engagement with the successful exchange of a product or service (and most importantly, that product or service delivers value to your client well beyond the price they paid).

In today's highly competitive business world, more often than not, it is the client, and not the seller who is the subject matter expert in their field. While this reality might be hard to accept from some, it is a reality none the less. The sales professional's role is not to be the industry expert who talks to their clients about feature, functions, and capabilities, but rather they are catalysts that help to quantify the value of goods and services, and to help the customer clearly see how and when that value will be realized. The client not only wants the sales team's help to confirm the value of products and services being proposed, but this value must be quantified in the context of their unique business. The customer will also be looking for a business transaction that results in at least a 2 to 1 financial return within the first year of making their investment. In other words, the customer will want

$2 of business value for every $1 of capital they spend with you, and they do not want to wait more than a year to realize this benefit.

As discussed in a previous chapter, the word "value" is an integral part of a sale professional's vocabulary. It is also an integral part of the sales professional's and sales managements' discussions about advancing the sales engagement. Using the Lean selling approach enables value to be quantified in the context of the customers' business problems that ultimately results in closing more sales. In terms of delivering a sales proposal to your client, it is vitally important to test your proposal for its value achieved compared to the capital outlay by the client. In Lean selling, the following client value realization model is used to test the value realized in comparison to the client's capital expenditure.

## Client Value Realization Model

$$\text{Value} = \left[\left(\frac{\text{benefit}}{\text{time}}\right) - \text{cost}\right] \times (1 - \text{risk}) \tag{8.1}$$

This model should be applied as a test early and often to qualify the health of the sales engagement and the proposal that is being developed. Testing the value proposition early and often improves sales planning and assists a sales professional to ensure that the sales engagement with the client is correctly focused on delivering a return on investment. To test that the business value delivered to the customer is worth more than their capital outlay for your products or services, the Lean selling client value realization model in Equation 8.1 focuses on four key elements of value:

1. **Business Benefit:** This component of the equation reflects the business outcome your client derives by eliminating the costly forms of Lean waste within their process after the seller's solution has been implemented. For example, as a result of successfully removing wastes, the business benefits that a client can quantify, resulting in a net operating savings or an increased competitive advantage due to improved operating efficiencies. Typically, the business benefits derived from the Lean selling methodology are based on delivering extrinsic value. Remember that extrinsic value is the portion of an item's net worth to a client that is assigned to it by external factors. These factors are typically

external to the product and service itself and relate to the client and their business outcomes that the product or service delivers. The sales focus while working with the value realization equation is to focus the sales plans on driving the business benefit up, such that the value realized by the client will increase proportionally.

2. **Capital Investment (Cost):** The total capital investment (cost) for the proposed product and services. These are the costs required to resolve client's problems and enable the achievement of their future state process. For true value to be present in the value proposition, the capital investment should be less than the business benefit realized by the customer once the product or service is consumed. The goal of the sales team while working with the value realization equation is to focus the sales plan on minimizing client costs such that value realized does not drop to a point where there is little or no net value to the client.
3. **Time:** Time relates to the proposed timeframe (time to value) by which the waste will be removed as a result of the successful delivery of the product and service. The goal of Lean selling is to deliver all or a major portion of the return within the first year of the product's service life. It is a vital component of value delivery that a sales proposal includes a plan that outlines the timeframe within which the wastes will be removed and business value will be realized. This proposed time frame enables the client to quantify the true value of the sale in the context of the time taken to deliver the net benefits compared with their capital investment. This tangible assessment is vital to the successful close of any sale. If the client cannot make the quantified assessment of value, then the sale probably will not close or it will be delayed. Therefore, the more detail that can be provided about time to value by way of a product delivery plan, then greater likelihood of closing the sale. When building a proposal based on time, the sales team should also focus on eliminating the 20% of the client's problems that will deliver to them 80% of the business value. Of course, the time to value should be delivered to the customer in the shortest possible time. While working with the value realization equation, the purpose is to minimize the time taken to eliminate the client's Lean wastes and deliver a business benefit, so that the value realized by the customers can be increased.
4. **Risk:** Risk is the likelihood that your product or service will NOT achieve the proposed business benefit and financial return to the client's business in the agreed timeframe. In the Lean selling conceptual model of value realization, the risk is typically measured as an agreed

weighting factor. It can be thought of as the inverse of a confidence level in delivering the solution on time, so when confidence is high, then risk is low. Risk is an important element in confirming value to a customer because clients are typically risk adverse (most of us are!). They must see their capital investment returned as quickly as possible. It is, therefore, vital that a client proposal to deliver value be quantified in the context of risk. If the risk is high, it could result in the Lean wastes not being removed and the client's business benefit not being delivered in the context of time and financial return. Alternatively, if the risk is high associated with a sales engagement, the sales organization should make a decision not to precede with a client engagement where it would be difficult to deliver value. After all, it is better to make this decision early rather than spend significant time and money on a sales engagement that in all likelihood will not close, or even worse, not exceed a client's expectation. It is important when using this Lean client value realization model that risk is reviewed throughout the project engagement. The risks associated with the sales engagement and product or services implementation will be dependent on number of factors and there are far too many to discuss here. The sales focus in working with the equation is to focus your sales plan on recognizing and mitigating project risk levels, as a high risk will reduce the realized value for a client. For example, if a sales project has a 50% risk of delivering the proposed value on time, then the value perceived by the client is cut in half. Conversely, if the seller is 99% confident (1% risk) that the entire business benefit will be realized on or before it is promised date, then the value as perceived by the client is only nominally reduced by risk.

By using Lean principles and the Lean selling methodology as an integral part of a sales engagement, a greater level of visibility and control regarding the project progression and potential risks is possible. Part of every Lean sales engagement involves the time taken to identify and quantify the root causes creating the client's problem. The more detail that is uncovered about a problem's root causes will increase a sales professional's ability to reduce and manage the risks that could impact a client's project. Risks will invariably have an impact on a project if they are not quantified or unknown. As the old adage goes, if you cannot measure it, then you cannot manage it. The same can be said for a project's risks. Lean selling provides insights and proper planning that ensures the project risks can be managed such that they do not impact the sales engagement or the proposed product implementation.

## *Client Value Realization Model Spreadsheet Formula*

As a final note on using the client value realization formula, a simple spreadsheet formula can be created to improve your sales engagement progression measurement. For this formula the arithmetic function is same as Equation 8.1.

While this formula is a conceptual model, the sales team can use throughout the sales engagement to model the projected client benefit as they work to qualify the sales opportunity and develop its final value proposition to the client. Lean for sales recommends that the final value proposal take the form of a Lean selling storyboard, which will be outlined in the next chapter.

# Chapter 9

# Bringing It All Together with the Lean Selling Storyboard

> If you can't explain it simply, you don't understand it well enough.
>
> **Albert Einstein**

## Making the Final Value Proposition to the Client

As with every chapter up to this point, we have cited a famous quotation from one of the world's most renowned scientific thinker, Albert Einstein, and this chapter is no exception. We begin this chapter with the Einstein quote, *"If you can't explain it simply, you don't understand it well enough."* What does that mean, especially in the context of Lean Selling and what does it have to do with Lean Story Telling by way of a Lean Selling Storyboard As the name "Storyboard" implies, the sales professional is telling a client's story from beginning to end. The storyboard has been build, shared, and improved upon starting from the very first client conversation. In the case of Lean Selling, it is the client's story about their journey of mutual discovery from "problem statement" to a "proposed solution." Along their journey, the client should have discovered the root cause, or causes, of their problem in addition to their recognizing the significant costs that this problem is having on their business. Now that all this work is complete, it is time to share this story with the key stakeholders throughout the client's business.

## The Need for Stakeholder Buy-In

The sales professional, who of course is leading the process of mutual discovery, now tells the client's story in a very logical fashion; so that not only the client appreciates the solution being proposed, but all other key stakeholders can easily "buy into" the Lean sales teams solution. For anyone who has attempted to make a change within a business—any size change both large and small—can attest to the fact that stakeholder "buy-in" is critical to getting that change adopted within the organization. Not only is stakeholder "buy-in" fundamental to implementing a new idea or proposal, but it is instrumental in sustaining that change as well. Without key stakeholder buy-in, and especially that of the leadership team of a business, a significant business change can be quickly undone by the next great idea. When business leaders are sufficiently invested in the decision process supporting a change, then adoption and longevity of that new idea is greatly improved. In this chapter, the simple yet effective technique of the Lean selling storyboarding is described.

In the world of sales these days, the technique of "story telling" is becoming more and more popular. Through traditional sales "story telling", the sales professional typically takes the prospective client on a verbal journey explaining in some detail how their proposed products or services have helped to deliver a tangible business outcomes for another client. The typical story consists of a use case of another client's critical business dilemma that ultimately culminates with a delighted client; whose business would not have survived otherwise, but if not for the sales professional's outstanding products and services. While the traditional storytelling approach may be interesting (and it may even be based on a client in a similar industry as the current client), the problem with a sales professional telling a story about another company is that it does not necessarily pertain to the problem of their current client. It most definitely is not personal to this new client, and it is usually subjective and does not help the client identify the extrinsic value that the sales professional's product will deliver to them. In fact, it will rarely pertain to a Lean sales professional's client because all clients' problems are unique and personal to them.

Remember, the most important Lean Selling Principle is that *value* is personal to the client. The Lean Selling Storyboard tells the client a story that is *personal* because it is *their* story. Fortunately for the Lean Sales Team, it is the story that you have just spent the last several weeks developing in cooperation and collaboration with your client. More importantly, for the client, it tells the story from problem identification through root cause to an ultimate solution that uniquely addresses the client's specific problem and cause, and delivers them business value.

## A Long Proposal versus a Short, Concise Lean Storyboard

Another common flaw with the traditional sales approach is the "sales proposal." It is not at all uncommon for a sales proposal to be a lengthy document—typically a word or text document—that can consist of over 30 pages, A typical sales proposal details the features, functions and financing options related to a seller's product offering. Ironically, most traditional sales proposals are not even read by the client; at least not in their entirety. To illustrate this point, the next time you or someone on your sales team hands a quote or bid proposal to your client, watch what he or she does next. Usually, they immediately take the document and quickly flick through it to find the page that includes your price. In Lean terms, all the other work on the traditional proposal can be considered Lean waste because it does not provide value from the client's perspective. This approach of verbose sales proposal writing has far outlived its usefulness. Even after all the hard work to compile a traditional sales proposal, it is not uncommon for the client to struggle to visualize how the documented solution will deliver value that is specific and personal to them. Fortunately, for the Lean sales professional, he or she has one final weapon in their arsenal; the *Lean Selling Storyboard.*

The Lean storyboard pulls the entire sales journey together into one comprehensive value proposition. The storyboard summarizes the Lean selling practices and all the relevant work products from the beginning of the journey, which you will recall started with the client's unique problem statement and concludes with the final value proposition that includes the all-important Time-to-Value (TtV) statement. A storyboard is typically a 4–8 page picture-based presentation that summarizes the client's Lean journey, and one of the unique benefits of this proposal is that the client will ultimately own it. It has been produced with the client and your sales team for the client. Once they are convinced of the proposed business value, the client can and will use it to convince their organization that the proposed solution is the right decision for their company – ultimately leading to a closed sale. In fact, the authors of this book have experience over three quarters of all Lean Selling storyboards results in a closed sale.

Looking back to our Lean sales funnel, we are now nearing the culmination of the sales cycle. We are making our comprehensive value proposition that outlines our Lean selling journey, and most importantly, tells the story from the client's perspective. In Figure 9.1, the Lean sales funnel is shown. As you can see, we are nearing the end of the client sales engagement, and we are anticipating with great confidence our moving forward and delivering on our value proposition.

By its very design, the funnel itself provides a useful framework for constructing our Lean sales storyboard. All the key work products from lean sales funnel steps are used to populate the storyboard. One of the benefits to following the Lean selling methodology is that very little effort is wasted on the part of the sales professional. Every part of the storyboard is produced for the client, with data from the client, and the final storyboard should ultimately help the client sell your solution internally. Remember, producing a document that is not valuable to a client is just another form of Lean waste. To that end, all of the collaborative work is very purposeful and leads to a solution that is relevant and real to your client. This Lean approach to sales, in and of itself, is a key differentiator for the sales professional.

The ability to quantify and align exactly how your products or services will eliminate the client's waste is unique and compelling and further differentiates you and your company from the competition. While the methodology is structured, it can be very straightforward and when the time comes to prepare the final value proposition, the majority of the work for completing the Lean selling storyboard has already been prepared. More importantly, it has already been validated by the client, so there are no misunderstandings or misgivings about what is being proposed and why it is being proposed.

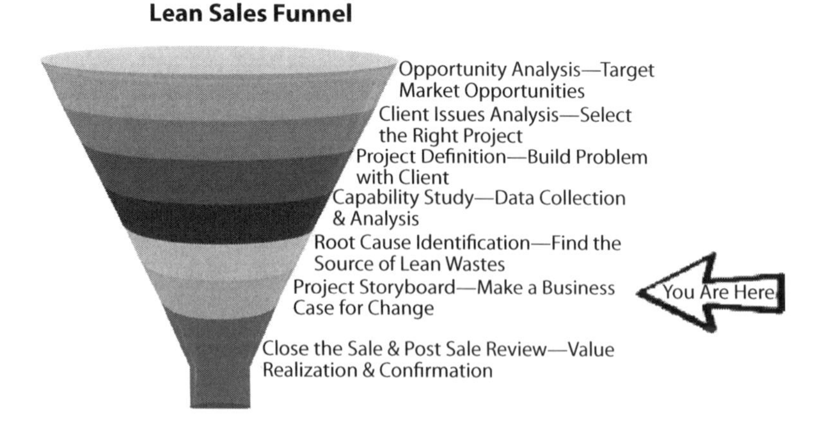


**Figure 9.1 The Lean sales funnel: project storyboarding (the value proposition).**

## Lean Selling Storyboard Outline

Below is an outline of a typical Lean selling storyboard:

1. Client problem statement and goal statement (using balanced scorecard success measures)
2. End-to-end process analysis (current state process map)
3. Process capability study
4. Root cause analysis
5. Future state process illustration
6. Time-to-value illustration
7. Solution proposal and business case quantification

### *Problem and Goal Statements*

To illustrate the Lean selling storyboard, let us use our The Gadget Shop scenario that we outlined in our previous chapter. Remember that The Gadget Shop is an online retailer who has a unique business challenge that we believe can be solved using our Lean selling techniques. After an initial meeting with the client the Lean seller drafts a problem and goal statement. Table 9.1 is an example of the problem and goal statement.

As you can see, the problem and goal are clearly stated in terms that are meaningful to the client, so that they are motivated to solve it. Within the context of the Lean selling storyboard the problem and goal statements remind the client just how big the problem really is. Further, the goal statement—along with the balanced scorecard success measures—quantifies the impact the problem is having on the client's business, and conversely it allows the client to see quite clearly the expected benefits that the Lean sales team's products and services will deliver.

The problem and goal statements are really the "book ends" of the Lean selling storyboard since the problem describes the client's current situation and the goal describes the desired future state, which is the "to-be state" that the Lean sales professional's products will deliver. When documenting the problem statement, remember its recommended construct, which is to clearly describe the client's current state compared with their desired state and to quantify the impact to the client's business as a result of this current problem. We call this construct the problem statement's "what" and "so what." In other words, "what" is the problem that we are trying to resolve

**Table 9.1 The Gadget Shop Problem and Goal Statement**

<table>
<tr><td colspan="2">Problem Statement:<br>The Gadget Shop is performing manual updates to their central stock and pricing database causing system inaccuracies that result in excessive inventories, costly increases in operating expenses, and a loss in revenue of approximately US$1.2M per annum.</td><td colspan="2">Goal Statement:<br>Perform real-time updates to the central stock and pricing database resulting improved inventory accuracy, reduced operating expenses, increased revenues, and improved client satisfaction metrics by year end. Achieving this goal will result annual saving of approximately US$1M in reduced operating expenses.</td></tr>
<tr><td>People Success Measures</td><td>Process Success Measures</td><td>Financial Success Measures</td><td>Customer Success Measures</td></tr>
<tr><td>A reduction in the procurement team correcting the central price file from 8 hr/wk to less than 1 hour resulting in less frustration of employees</td><td>A reduction in procurement correcting the central price file from 8% to less than 1% resulting in less frustration of employees</td><td>Realize a financial impact of over US$1M per annum, as a result of lower operating costs and increased revenue over our prior year</td><td>Reduce customer complaints due to delays from over 20% of those visiting our website to 2% or below</td></tr>
</table>

and the "so what" is the impact to their business if you can help them solve it.

Also, remember that the goal statement should follow the specific-measurable-achievable-relevant-time-based criteria (S-M-A-R-T). Both the sales professional and the client need to know what success looks like. In other words, how will we know that we solved this problem? Hence, the goal must be specific and measurable, so that everyone agrees with its proposed outcome as being realized. The sales professional's products or services should align to enable the goal, as promised. The "achievable" criteria may be a challenge for some in sales, but it is critically important not to "over sell" or over commit. It is oftentimes tempting to proclaim that our products and services can solve all of the client's problems (and at the same time solve world hunger!), but it is rarely realistic that 100% of the client's pains will be eliminated by way of one particular sale. The sales professional using Lean selling should be aggressive yet realistic when setting goals, so that they maintain credibility in the eyes of the client.

### *Storyboards Are a Stand-Alone Document*

The Lean selling storyboard is intended to be a "stand-alone" document—meaning that if the sales professional was not available—then the storyboard can "speak for itself" and stand-alone on its own merit. Typically, a Lean storyboard is built on the customer's corporate logo template, using their corporate colors, and is built collaboratively with the client and their team. It is subsequently presented back to the client and key stakeholders by the sales team with the addition of the sales team's proposed solution to eradicate the client's waste. Additionally, your customer contact and key sponsors now have a storyboard they can be used during ongoing internal discussions that are personal to their business. Having this clear, concise and complete proposal makes the storyboard hugely valuable in terms of gaining internal buy-in from multiple client stakeholders. Working in this way significantly increases the sales team's likelihood of closing a sale.

## ***End-to-End Process Analysis***

Illustrating a client's problem in terms of their own process, once again, makes the Lean selling approach unique and effective. Since "value" is personal to every client, it is critical to make a "value proposition" that is personal to the client. This value proposition is the Lean selling storyboard itself, and illustrating a client's current state process by way of a value stream map (VSM) is the foundation of the storyboard. Depicting the client's process in a clear and accurate way through a VSM helps the client to visualize problems within the context of how the various forms of Lean wastes are impacting business. For example, the "cascade effect" that documents the cumulative impact of a client's Lean waste, should come across loud and clear via the client's current state VSM.

Another benefit of the leveraging a VSM in the storyboard is that it represents a common language that can be used to highlight the problem and its impact on the client's entire business. All of the key decision makers (those making or influencing the decision to purchase) can relate to what the storyboard is telling them because it represents their process and their business—and more importantly—it highlights their unique problems. Even though they have probably never seen their end-to-end business processes illustrated in such a way, the CEO, CFO, COO, and others on the client's team will relate to the VSM and what it is telling them, which is that they have a lot of Lean waste within their business processes and it is having a detrimental impact on overall business performance. Figure 9.2 illustrates a current state VSM for The Gadget Shop.

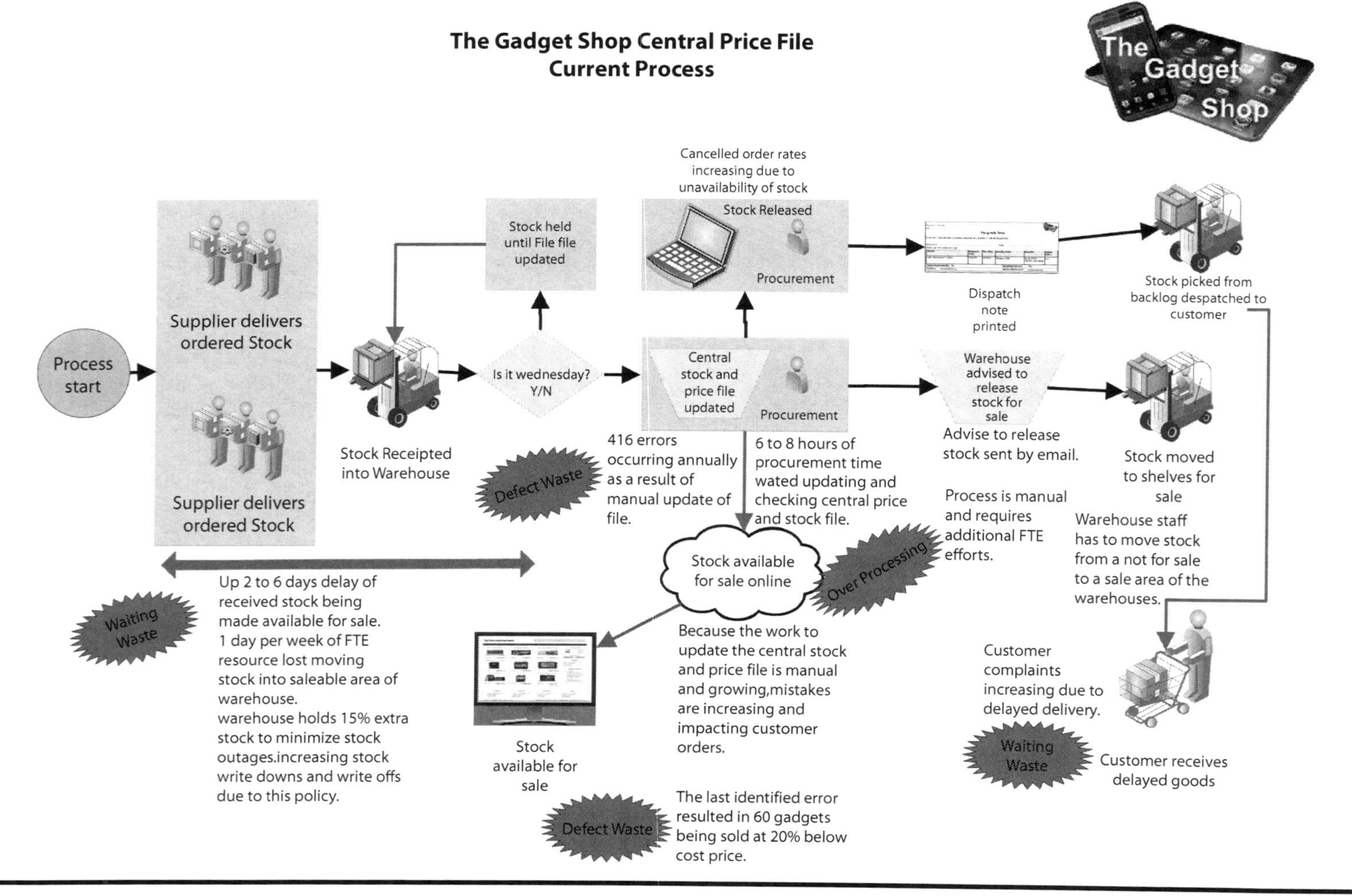


**Figure 9.2 The Gadget Shop's "As-Is" or current state process map illustrating the forms of destructive Lean wastes.**

## *Kaizen Bursts Indicate Improvement and Sales Opportunities*

Notice that in the current state VSM, there are a number of "kaizen bursts." These are the explosion-like symbols that denote the various forms of Lean wastes that are present in the current process. They also indicate where they are located within the client's process. Like most of the Lean terminology, the word "kaizen" is a Japanese term and loosely translates into "change for the better." (*kai—means to break apart, and zen—means good or better; so kaizen means to break something apart and put it back together even better.*) A kaizen burst represents an improvement opportunity that exists within the "As-Is" process, and in a traditional Lean improvement program the burst would denote a potential area for a kaizen event, where a self-directed work team from the client's organization would address this situation. For the sales professional, it represents an opportunity to eliminate, or at least minimize, the destructive effect that this Lean waste is having by virtue of delivering a product or service to the client that addresses the kaizen opportunity.

At this point, the sales professional is working to align the offerings in their portfolio that can help the client solve the problem, although it is not quite time to present those solutions to the client. It is important that the sales professional first spends a little more time talking about the client's problems and the impact they are having on business.

## ***Client Capability Study***

The client capability study was described in detail in Chapter 7 and now is the time to summarize the client's process capability in the context of the Lean storyboard. A good time to present the capability study is right after describing the current state (As-Is) VSM and identifying the various forms of Lean waste that are present in the process. The capability study attempts to quantify the impact that these wastes are having on the client's business. When the sales professional quantifies the impact of a client's problem(s), they are setting the stage to make the business case for a proposed solution to the problem(s), as the financial consequence of the Lean wastes is communicated to the client (in many cases for the first time). Table 9.2 is an example of a capability study summary that would be included into the Lean storyboard presentation. In The Gadget Shop example, it is clear that the impact of holding 15% extra inventory is costing their business around US$1.2M. The reason why The Gadget Shop needs to hold this excess inventory has yet to be presented, and leads the sales professional to the next storyboard topic, which is the Root Cause Analysis.

**Table 9.2 Illustrating the Capability Study Performed on The Gadget Shop Process**

| *Identified Outcomes of Problems* | *Measurement Category* | *Measurement Units* | *Measurement System* |
|---|---|---|---|
| The policy of holding 15% extra stock is costing the company US$100,000 a month in increased operating costs. Additionally, due to increased cash flow on occasions the company incurs interest on an overdraft as a result of insufficient liquid funds to pay for new stock at time of ordering. | Hard Dollar | Increased operating costs | USD |
| Reduction in gross margins impacts company profitability as a result of increased frequency of stock write offs. | Hard Dollar | Increased stock write off and revenue loss | USD |
| Errors in entering price and stock details resulted in products being sold below cost sold price. Sales had to be honored and resulted in 60 gadgets sold at 20% below. | Hard Dollar | Loss of sales | USD |

## Root Cause Analysis

Every problem solver recognizes the importance of getting beyond symptoms and reaching the true source of a problem. Far too often, however, only the symptoms of a problem get addressed in an interest to achieve a quick resolution. Everyone who has ever experienced a significant business problem is eager to get past the problem and return to a trouble-free state; so there is oftentimes lot of pressure placed on the problem solver(s) to resolve the problem as quickly as possible. Sometimes, the problem solver does not feel they have the time to solve the problem properly, so they rush to a solution. A hasty solution almost always fails to find the problem's root cause, thus the problem resurfaces and its impacts continue to plague a business.

Just about every client has been guilty of "symptoms solving" at one time or another. This results in the client failing to permanently and effectively solving their problems. This situation creates an opportunity for sales professionals to lead the client in identifying the root cause or causes of the business problems that are plaguing them. Root cause analysis is an opportunity for sales professionals to differentiate themselves from other sales professionals in that they identify the source of problems that are unique to their clients, and this opens the door for a solution that provides unparalleled value to clients. In Figures 9.3 and 9.4, the sales team has built two Ishikawa, or fishbone, diagrams that help to identify the root causes of the client's problem. The Lean sales professional created a 6M fishbone diagram, and a technical sales professional created a 5S fishbone diagram with the client's IT since they were analyzing a transactional or systems process. Interestingly, both Ishikawa diagrams identify the same root cause, which is a good validation that the real root cause was identified.

Also, notice that the fishbone diagram consists of the "5-Why Analysis" that is used in conjunction with the Ishikawa diagram to help the sales professional to delve past symptoms in order to surface root causes. The "actionable" root causes are also highlighted in the diagram. These are the causes that will be "actioned" by the sales team via a product or service that will address these causes.

Once again, this approach is very personal and unique to the client. The sales professional's proposed solutions address the specific problems and their causes that are unique to that client's business. This is just another way that Lean selling is helping sales professionals differentiate themselves from the rest of the field.

While the sales professional has a solution (or solutions) that can and will address these root causes, the seller first presents what the new business process will look like once these root causes are addressed. While this book will refer to the next section of the Lean storyboard as the "Future State" process map, the seller may also choose to depict the "Ideal State" process, which is what the client's business process can look like if all the Lean wastes are removed. While the sales professional will only address some of the Lean wastes during this particular sales proposal, the ideal process map creates a vision that the client and sales professional can work on for the next several years. As soon as the time is right for the client, the stage has been set to address the other Lean wastes and their causes.

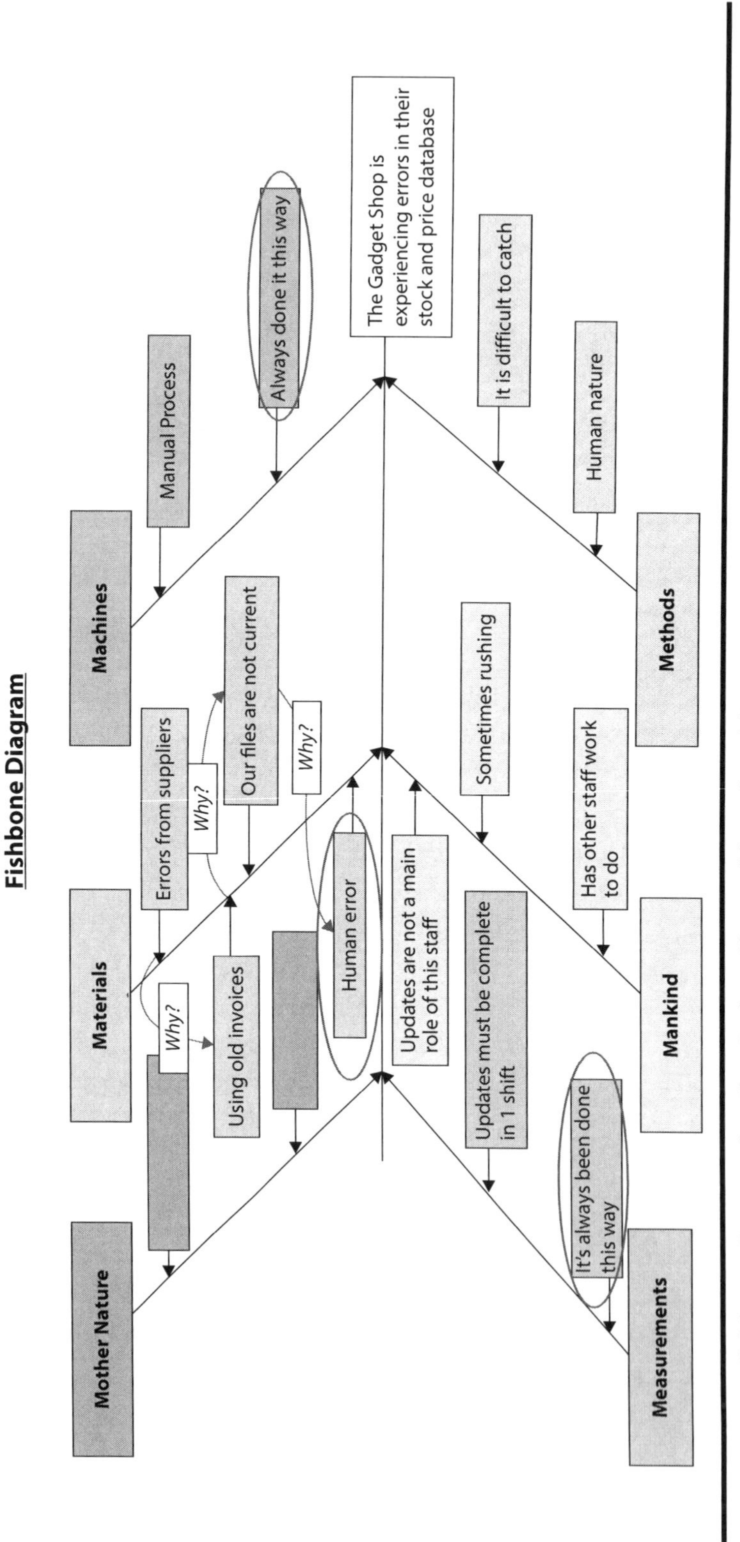


**Figure 9.3 A fishbone diagram for The Gadget Shop with actionable root causes (with traditional 6M cause categories).**

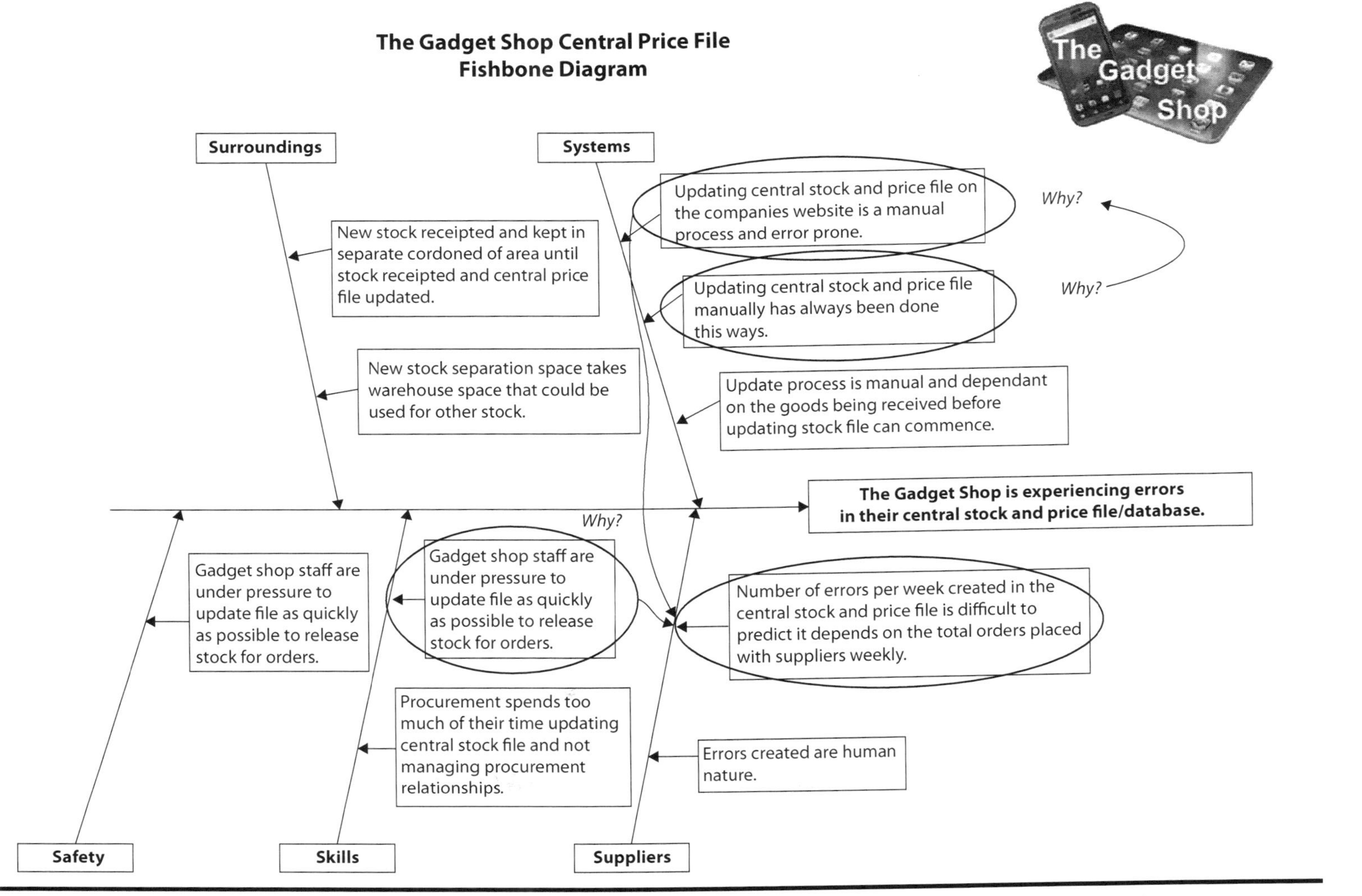


**Figure 9.4** A fishbone diagram for The Gadget Shop with actionable root causes (with Service cause categories)

## Future State Process Illustration

The sales professional will now shift his focus to portraying to the client how an ideal process might look. So presenting the future state, or "To-Be," process usually follows the "fishbone diagram" in the Lean selling storyboard, since a thorough analysis of the current state process has been effectively presented to the client. Here, the sales team describes what the client's business processes can look like without the various forms of Lean wastes that reside in the process and has been cleansed of all their destructive downstream effects. Figure 9.5 depicts an illustration of a future state VSM for The Gadget Shop's web-based ordering process.

Notice in the future state VSM that there are no more Kaizen Bursts since the sales team was able to address all the ill-effects caused by manually updating the central price and stock file. It is important to point out that, this new and improved process does not mean that the sales professionals products were able to totally eradicate all the problems in the client's process, but rather the sales team paints a realistic picture of what they believe their products can do in terms of addressing the client's problems. More times than not, the client is delighted with the proposed "To-Be" process as it is dramatically improving the client's business outcomes. Once again, the sales person momentarily leaves the client on a hanging note, as they have not yet told the client how and when this new process will become a reality. Coming next is the long awaited "Time to Value" (TtV) illustration that follows the future state VSM presentation.

## Time to Value Illustration

Now, the stage has been adequately prepared to outline the Lean selling solution to the client's problem. First, a business problem has been identified and its impact has been thoroughly quantified and monetized. Then, the Lean wastes and their root causes have been identified in the current process, and in addition, the future state of the client's business has been aptly described. Now, it is time to outline the Lean sales professional solutions along with the ever important "TtV." In previous chapters, the authors described relevance of TtV in the world of sales, and most importantly, its relevance to the client. Here is the time and place within the Lean Storyboard to illustrate the TtV for this specific client problem.

Figure 9.6 shows an example of the TtV graphic that is shared with The Gadget Shop executives. Here, not only is the seller demonstrating that he

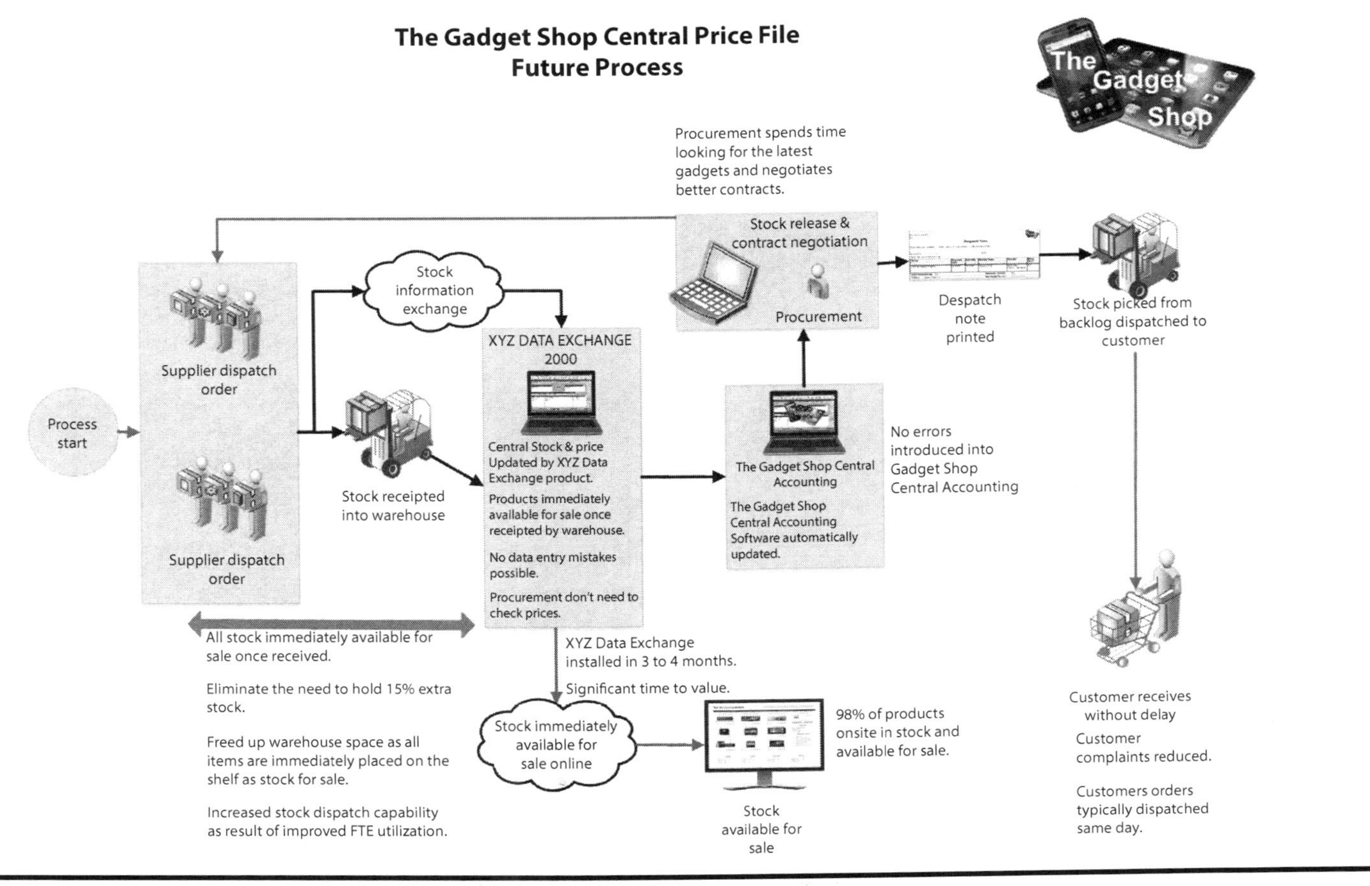


**Figure 9.5 The Gadget Shop's "To-Be" or future state process map illustrating the Lean waste-free process.**

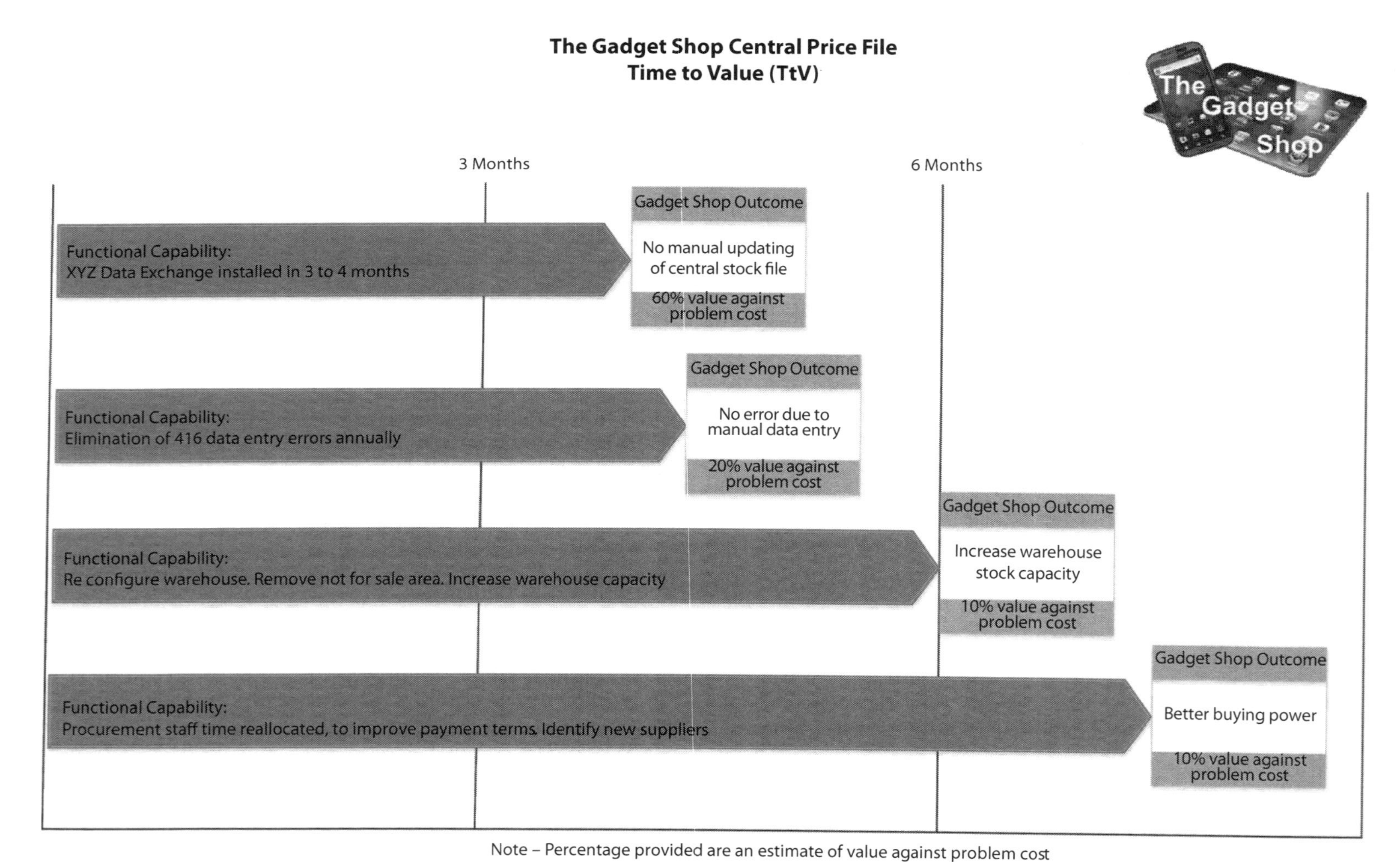


**Figure 9.6 A graphic illustrating the Time to Value chart for The Gadget Shop client.**

or she has a solution that addresses the client's problems, but more importantly, the seller is demonstrating TtV. The sales professional is illustrating the "Pareto Principle" for Lean selling in the TtV chart, which is to provide a solution that addresses 80% of the client's problems as quickly as possible. This is the point in the proposal where a sales professional outlines the portfolio of products and services to enable the client's Future State. In other words, what is the 20% of functionality enabled by your product and services that will eliminate 80% of the client's key wastes in the shortest possible time. Ideally, these wastes should be eliminated in 3 months, 6 months, and 9 months following the close of the sale and may require a portfolio of products to accomplish the desired outcomes. This timing should be clearly outlined as in Figure 9.5. More importantly, it should be clear to the client why the sales professional is recommending this approach. Of course, longer range solutions can be recommended; however, to make your storyboard a compelling reason for the client to buy, a Lean sales professional shows the client stakeholders how net operating costs will be reduced within that timeframe. The net saving can then offset the capital acquisition cost made by the client. The unique feature of a TtV chart is that the 3 to 6 month solution set can provide the return on investment (ROI) that helps to fund even longer range solutions. This self-funding approach can ultimately help the client achieve their Future State process, and puts them well on the path to a process free of the deadly forms of Lean waste.

## Building a Business Case for Change

In this case, The Gadget Shop is experiencing a significant reduction in operating expenses that needs to be quantified and illustrated; however, a business case could also showcase an increase in revenue or a market share gain for the client. Since our Time to Value (TtV) chart illustrates how value is delivered to the client over time, the Lean sales team will break down their financial returns into the shortest time intervals possible. In The Gadget Shop example, the TtV shows that the team's solution returns are delivered in a 3 to 9 month timeframe. Figure 9.7 illustrates how the solution will be implemented to deliver a favorable client return over time. In using the Lean Selling approach the sales team identified the following opportunities for The Gadget Shop:

Manually updating the central price and stock file has resulted in The Gadget Shop purchasing 15% extra stock to keep up with customer demand. This form of Lean Inventory waste is costing the company $1,200,000 per

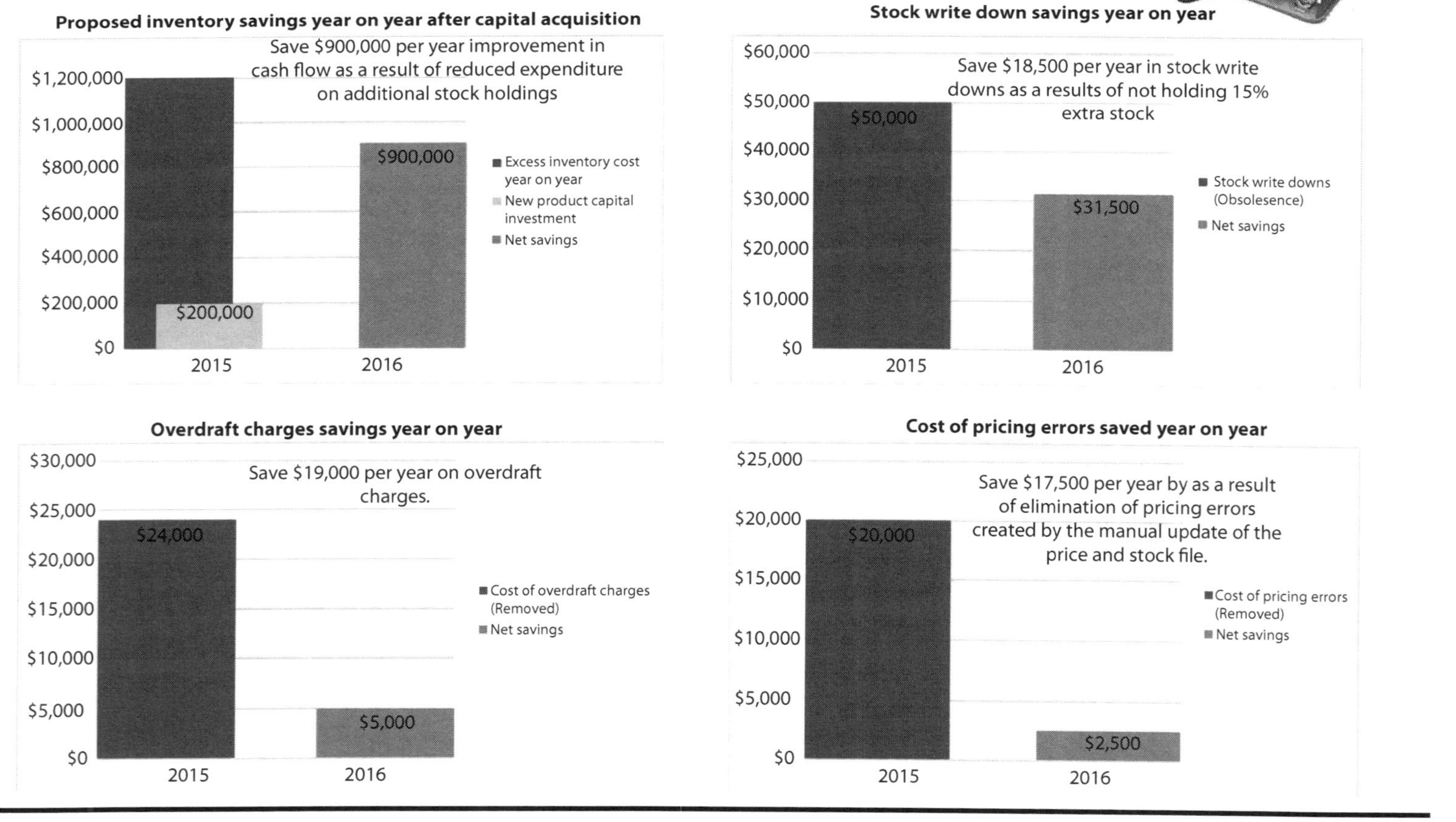


**Figure 9.7 An illustration of the financial benefits business case for The Gadget Shop storyboard.**

annum in increased operating costs. Additionally, the company has seen an increase in the amount of stock having to be sold off as clearance items once new gadgets become available. These price mark downs are costing the company $50,000 per annum, and of course a reduction in profit margins on many of their popular gadgets. Furthermore, the company had a pricing error last year that cost the company $20,000 in reduced sales and profit margins.

The Lean sales team has decided that their XYZ Data Exchange will automate the updates to the central price and stock information in The Gadget Shops accounting system. Delivering this outcome eradicates the Over Processing Waste of spending between 6 and 8 hours per week to manually update the central price and stock file. Additionally, it will eliminate manual data entry errors that resulting in stock being sold below cost (Defect Waste). Most importantly, it will eliminate the need for The Gadget Shop to hold 15% extra stock. The implementation of the XYZ Data Exchange at The Gadget Shop will take the sales team 3 months to "go live" with this solution. The Data Exchange costs $200,000 to purchase and install. After installing it, The Gadget Shop will save over $100,000 per month in operating costs. As well, this improvement will significantly reduce the amount of product sold as clearance stock, and consequently The Gadget Shop will realize between $2000 and $4000 per month in improved profit margins.

Based on the information uncovered by the customer and the sales team, the TtV of the proposed solution will be delivered in 5 to 6 months with the $200,000 capital investment realizing a 2 month payback period after installation. Capital funding is achieved as a result of The Gadget Shop no longer needing to hold 15% extra stock. This time to value exceeds our standard of a $2 of return for every $1 of spend by the client. In addition to the hard savings there are a number of soft returns delivered in terms of TtV. The first benefit is the elimination of 416 manual data entry errors each year. The XYZ Data Exchange fully automates this function and removes the possibility of human error. The second outcome of the proposed solution is that within 3 months of delivering this solution the dedicated "Not for Sale" area in the warehouse is no longer required. This valuable floor space can be reallocated for revenue generating inventory and new product lines. The third and final TtV benefit is the fact that within 6 months of using the XYZ Data Exchange the Procurement team will be able to refocus 6 to 8 hours of non-value added activity on new value added activities like finding new suppliers and negotiating better payment terms for The Gadget Shop.

Obviously our Gadget Shop example is a fictitious company and some readers may be thinking "It is easy to build a business case when the business scenario and financial numbers are all made up!" If you are thinking the same thing, remember that the authors have created a simplistic business case to make it easier for you to understand the important principles of Lean selling. Also, please don't lose sight of the fact that during our actual sales engagements, we truly do spend sufficient time quantifying the client's problem in the context of their Lean wastes and the business impact resulting from the cascade effect. The Gadget Shop illustration is very typical of a Lean selling engagement. Value delivery is made possible by spending time identifying root causes, process mapping the current state and quantifying the real costs of Lean waste. Lean Selling is not a theory, but rather a sales methodology that has been successfully applied with real customers over a period of many years; resulting in dozens of very satisfied clients.

However the Lean sales professional and client prefer to see the business benefit, it is important to quantify all of the hard and soft benefits that the client's business can expect to realize from their purchase. Figure 9.7 illustrates the difference operating costs and projected savings that The Gadget Shop will realize once their Lean wastes are eradicated by way of the sales team's proposed solution.

Now, the Lean selling storyboard presentation is almost complete. Of course, a summary slide or Q&A slide at the end of the presentation is an appropriate way to conclude the discussion. Once the presentation is complete, the sales engagement moves into the final negotiations and closing phase. Another benefit of having a clear, complete, and concise storyboard is that the client (the seller's direct contact) can and often will use the presentation to make the proposal to other decision makers within their business. There is no better compliment to the Lean sales professional than when his/her client uses the completed storyboard to help close the sale by presenting it to the other key decision makers within their own business.

## Storyboarding Makes Decision Making Easier

One final benefit of the Lean selling storyboard is that it provides objective business performance measurements that both the client and the seller can use to substantiate whether or not the sales teams solution delivered the projected benefits. In the traditional sales world, the sales professional moves on to work on the next engagement once a deal is closed. This approach is a big mistake, because once your product's proposed value has been documented and confirmed, then your client's likelihood to recommend your organization increases

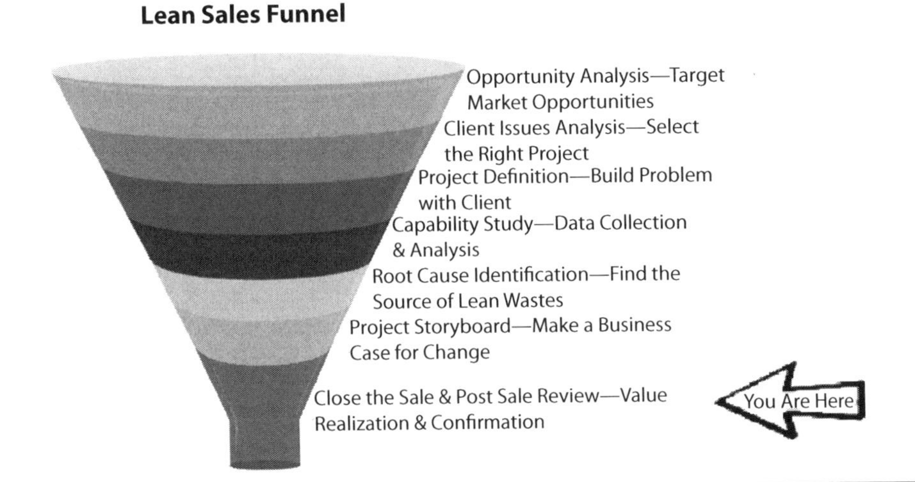


**Figure 9.8 Illustration of the Lean sales funnel highlighting the last stage.**

significantly. This situation in turn leads to a client to "pull" more sales projects from your company based on the business relationship that you've just built. As all good Lean practitioners know, a "push" transaction is never desirable between a customer and their supplier, but rather achieving a "pull" between the client and Lean sales organization is consistent with core Lean principles. With the Lean selling approach, once the sales professional validates the business value delivered to client, they have earned the right to stay engaged and deliver more value. You are now considered a trusted advisor to your client and as long as your engagements continue to focus on Lean principles and value delivery then a collaborative relationship will endure. Lean selling is a professional sales approach that is designed to place the client's needs above those of the sales organization. It is this reason that makes it so effective. To complete our Lean for Sales cycle, Figure 9.8 illustrates the culmination of our journey by identifying the final stage of the Lean sales funnel; where value is delivered to client and confirmed by the sales professional.

## Close the Sale & Confirm Client Value—Value Realization

Now that the value proposition has been delivered to the client by way of the Lean selling storyboard, we are now at the phase in the Lean sales funnel where the sales professional will close the sale and confirm that value has been delivered to the client. In terms of closing the sale with the client, typically there is really no traditional closing process. In other words, based on the authors' experience there is little or no bargaining back and forth, nor is there any debating as to the selection of the appropriate products and services that will truly deliver value to the client. Since the Lean sales professional has been co-creating the value proposition with the client, and performing continuous qualification every step of the way, then the only closing process that takes place is the client selling the value proposition within their own organization. The Lean storyboard makes it easy for the client to sell the proposal to other key stakeholders and decision makers in their business. The role of the Lean sales professional is to support the client's internal sales process in any and every way that the client requires. For example, the client may request the Lean sales professional present the storyboard to other key stakeholders in the client's organization, and/or the sales team may need to describe or demonstrate how a proposed product or service specifically addresses the root cause of the client's business problem.

This closing process is a refreshing change from the historical approach where the client and sales representative may have traditionally sat across the table and negotiated back and forth on the details of certain terms and conditions of the sale. Much of this traditional negotiating emanates from the client's skepticism that the seller will actually deliver the value they are promising. Of course, the client will always try to get the best deal for their business, and by providing a solid business case by way of the Lean selling storyboard the sales professional ensures that the client is solving their unique problem, and at the same time they substantiate their return on investment.

More to the point of ensuring a very favorable return on investment for the client, the Lean sales professional must confirm the value that their solutions ultimately deliver to the client. The Lean approach to selling makes this value confirmation a very objective process. Using The Gadget Shop as an example, the Lean sales professional proposed a product that will electronically transfer the stock and file details from the Gadget suppliers; hence eliminating the need to manually update the central inventory system. There was a specific business benefit associated with the client's adoption of this new product, and the Lean sales professional can validate that the projected cost reductions were actually realized by The Gadget Shop. When the Lean sales professional contacts their client to confirm that business value was actually realized, not only is the client impressed as some traditional sellers may never confirm the that value has been delivered by their products and services, but it also bolsters the Lean sales professional's reputation as an associate who truly cares about the client's business. Once again, the Lean sales professional's role of the trusted advisor to their client is solidified.

# Chapter 10

# Conclusion and a Call to Action

> The whole of science is nothing more than a refinement of everyday thinking.
>
> **Albert Einstein**

Throughout this book, we have emphasized the need to combine the art and science of selling to proactively address the client needs. Also, we have discussed the need to interject Lean thinking and its practices in the sales world to not only better understand the client's needs, but to also improve the value that your products deliver to your clients. We have also focused on strategies to help you understand the concepts behind the Lean thinking as it is applied to sales; as well as the applicability of the key Lean selling practices to a sales engagement. Now is the time that we need to encourage you to apply the concepts and practices that you have just learned.

As with any new learning, there is a need to apply what you learned quickly into a real-life application. This book has been created by the authors to challenge sales organizations everywhere to begin using Lean principles to methodically increase the "scientific thinking" and Lean selling practices as an every day approach to your next sales engagement. You also need to revisit your current sales model, and start with a mind-set of Lean thinking by asking yourself —"How can I make our sales engagements more personal to the client and more scientific in our approach?"

In an earlier chapter, we talked in detail about managing stakeholders and aligning your product or service to their individual and personal requirements.

By utilizing the Lean selling approach you are going to generate value and reduce the time to deliver that value to your client. Keep in mind, however, that there could be some resistance from the client's organization when you first approach them with a Lean selling engagement. Remember that initially they will not be used to this approach, and possibly even skeptical about your true intentions. They may be concerned that it requires too much work on their end to help you make a sale. Do not get discouraged, instead, give them an overview of this approach; while letting them know that you will be leading this effort for them, and you will make them an integral part of the value generation process. Ultimately, their confidence in you and the Lean approach will increase as they start to see results, especially when all the other key stakeholders in the client's organization begin seeing result as well. You may be already an expert in applying the "art and know-how" of selling, but be open to the fact that applying some more "science" to how you currently approach sales can never be a disadvantage.

Surely, all of us have seen over the years where there has been a significant positive impact when adding some science and rigor to the way we approach our work. In particular, when we are trying to solve a problem then it is a fact-based, data-driven approach that always delivers superior results compared with a less structured approach. You will surely find a similar positive impact when you begin integrating the art of sales with the science of Lean (i.e. Lean selling) The Lean selling approach will have a dramatic impact on any sale professional's close rates; which will be many multiple times of where they are today. Furthermore, this approach will transcend you beyond the role of the traditional seller to a role that is much more valuable in the eyes of your client. Lean selling will transform your current client relationship and position you as their trusted advisor.

The most important step at this point is your first engagement with a client to introduce the Lean selling approach. You may have heard the ancient Chinese proverb: "A journey of a thousand miles begins with a single step." Getting started is always the hardest part of any change effort. Challenge yourself to take that all-important first step. Make your next client engagement a Lean selling engagement, and start that new sales cycle with the principle of giving. For example, bring your client a problem and goal statement based on some publicly available information that you have researched about your client's industry in preparation for your initial sales call. The problem statement does not even have to be perfect. In fact, you want to have a meaningful discussion around the information that you've prepared; so discussing how your problem statement can be improved to more accurately represent a client's unique business challenge is exactly what you want to have happen during your initial client meeting. This discussion is a conversation well worth having, and from a Lean selling perspective it would be considered a very successful first sales call, as you have just completed your very first hypothesis test (i.e. continuous qualification) with your client.

At the end of your first trial run, conduct a "lessons learned" with your sales team and with your client. Ask them, "What went well?," "What could be different?," and "What ideas are there for improving future Lean selling approaches?" Do not get de-motivated if the first round does not go exactly as planned. Simply solicit feedback from your client, your key stakeholders and your team, and then use this feedback to help chart your next steps. A Lean sales professional should always view feedback as a gift; and especially feedback from a client. Lean principles teach us to capitalize on opportunities for continuous improvement and to make any necessary adjustments before our next client engagement (in other words, make the necessary course corrections and always look for ways to improve the way we engage with our client). A Lean sales professional should take full advantage of any client engagement to learn and improve by soliciting key stakeholder feedback and acting upon it.

First of all, don't dismiss any of the techniques outlined in this book without first trying them. It is far too easy to assume that a tool or technique is not worth the time and effort needed to utilize it. These Lean selling practices require just that—"practice" by the sales professional and team in order to perfect the disciplines outlined in this book and to make them your own. Consider the ancient philosophy of Aikido martial art masters who teach the *Shuhari* approach to students learning a new practice. For those not familiar with this philosophy, the concepts of "Shu-Ha-Ri" loosely translates from their ancient oriental origins to "learn-detach-transcend"; which means that at first a practitioner must follow the practices exactly as prescribed, and once the practices become second nature then the practitioner can step back and adapt these practices to their particular context or situation. The same principle of *Shuhari* applies to Lean selling in that everyone should try each and every practice as outlined in this book, and if over time there is a need to customize or modify them, then the Lean sales professional has the needed experience and insights to be able to adapt these practices most effectively.

Our hope is that anyone and everyone can utilize Lean selling techniques and quickly apply them with great success. Once you have mastered them, then you should feel free to modify them to make them work for you and your sales team; and most importantly for your particular client. The tools and templates outlined in this book are simply tools and techniques that should work for you and not vice-versa. One should never become a slave to a template and once you fully understand their purpose, then you should always feel empowered to modify them to help solve your unique business problem. Also, when you are with a client using these techniques and it feels like you are force fitting a tool or technique, then simply don't do it. Instead, you should try another structured approach that accomplishes the desired purpose. For example, if you are trying to identify a root cause with your client and an Ishikawa diagram does not seem appropriate, then simply lead your client and sales team in a 5-Why discussion. The important point here is that you need to move the team beyond symptoms in order to address a root cause with your sales proposal, and there are a number of ways for accomplishing this objective. Remember that regardless of which phase of the Lean sales funnel you are operating within, a fact-based and data-driven approach will always deliver superior client outcomes compared with other less objective alternatives. While using the Lean selling approach, always keep in mind that your goal is to generate value for your client, as quickly and effectively as possible.

We are confident that by applying the concepts presented in this book, your Lean selling skills will become your edge over other sellers. Not only are you able to proactively identify business improvement opportunities for your clients while closely collaborating with them; but you are generating value much more quickly for them (in other words, you are their trusted advisor). Most important, you are learning valuable skills that are scalable and portable to any industry domain. The techniques presented in this book have been tried and tested across many business domains and have never failed to deliver impressive results.

In summary, there is a tremendous amount of transformation happening across the world—irrespective of the domain you are currently working in—your business is probably undertaking some form of significant change. Organizations are forced to become more lean, nimble, and agile, so that they can respond to their clients' needs much more quickly. To continue your personal transformation, recognize that data (unstructured and structured) is the world's newest natural resource and decisions need to made as quickly as possible by utilizing this vast resource. You will quickly see how leveraging data can open your client's eyes to where, when and how they can realize significant business value by way of harvesting and disseminating this new knowledge across their business. Your client will soon realize this approach is an important key to their ongoing business success.

Lean selling is an excellent enabler to all the aforementioned challenges. We are able to use data to make meaningful decisions, Lean techniques to remove the wastes out of the process, understand what value means to clients and deliver it to them quickly. If a sales professional after reading this book does not apply these Lean principles and practices, then someone else surely will, and when they do, they will quickly learn and confirm the benefits that Lean's formal approach delivers to their sales quota. As with most of these disciplines, practice makes perfect. Keep trying to apply these methods in your sales engagements until you master these skills, and most importantly, keep thinking—how can I make this better? This challenge will keep you motivated in your long and successful Lean selling journey, and a successful sales career!

Finally, it is not the intent of this book to make you a Lean consultant. Outlined in these chapters are fundamental problem solving and process improvement practices that are time tested and guaranteed to be effective. Just as important as their effectiveness is the ease of use of these techniques. Almost anyone having read this book can apply these methods for the betterment of their profession, and ultimately to the delight of their client. And now, we will close this chapter and conclude this book in the same manner that we started it, with a famous expression from the scientific mind of Albert Einstein who said, "A person who never made a mistake has never tried anything new." Now, go out there and give Lean selling a try … you have nothing to lose and a client's trust to gain!

# Index

## O



## P



## R



## S



## T

## U



## V



## W